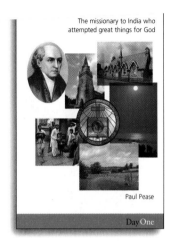

The missionary to India who
attempted great things for God

Paul Pease

Day One

Series Editor: Brian H Edwards

Day One

TRAVEL WITH

William **Carey**

Ignited by Cook

William Carey began to bring his powerful mind captive to God's word. This enabled him to persevere during the most severe trials, and led him to begin dreaming big dreams for God

Having found new life in Christ, Carey now had some big issues to think through. He began to engage his soul youthful, yet rigorous and well-ordered, mind to sorting out some of the implications of his new life. Which church should he join? He had been attending the prayer meetings at Hackleton during the week, but the parish church on Sundays. He found more spiritual help from the Dissenters (a title for any Protestant group not in the Church of England) but they were at that time belittled, counted as socially inferior to Anglicans, and discriminated against. To join them would damage his social standing. He also felt some loyalty to the Church of England as both his grandfather and his father had been parish clerks. To which community of believers should he belong? It was not an easy decision.

Carey made his choice on Sunday 10 February 1779. King George III proclaimed this day as a day of national fasting and prayer because of the bad turn of events for the British in the

COBBLER & TEACHER

Above: The second panel in Moulton's Mural depicting Carey as Cobbler and Teacher and showing the Moulton cottage—Teaching—Shoe making and repairs—Nichols' cottage interior

facing page: St John the Baptist church, Piddington, where Dorothy Carey was christened on 25 January 1756, and where she later married William in June 1781

Above: The ancient and modern in today's India. The ox and its cart would have been a familiar sight to Carey

Left: Street market life, little changed from Carey's day

Over the past sixteen months Dorothy had suffered many hardships, hurts, losses and fears: the sad and frantic farewells in England, the long voyage with a young baby, the culture shock of India, the uncertainty of the numerous moves, the humiliation and pain of dysentery, her sister left in Debhata, and now the death of her five year old son. It all became too much for her, and she seemed to retreat from reality. When she contracted serious dysentery again sometime between January and March 1795 Dorothy plummeted deep into a mental illness that stayed with her up to her death twelve years later in 1807.

Dorothy had 'slipped across the subjective border between sanity and insanity.' She could be quite rational with some people and at some times, but then she would break into violent and abusive outbursts as she raged against William. During these occasions her language could become obscene, and she became highly suspicious of her husband, stalking him from place to place and openly accusing him of unfaithfulness. She even threatened to cut his throat with a kitchen knife. William wrote home to his sisters: 'My poor wife must be considered as insane, and is the occasion of great sorrow.' William and John Thomas

wondered what to do, they tried various strategies to help her, but eventually, and reluctantly, they had to confine her to her room during those bouts of irrationality. A clinical psychologist, James Beck, has written: 'Today we would diagnose Dorothy's condition as a Delusional Disorder or Paranoid Disorder-Jealous Type.' During her illness William did not always react as he

A reality check for those back home

In order for his home supporters to understand how hard his task was, Carey wrote the following words: 'Only imagine England to be in the situation of Bengal;

without public roads, inns, or other convenience for travel; without post, save for the letters of the nobility; without the boon of printing, and absorbed in the monkish superstition of the eleventh century— that in this situation two or three men across from

Greenland to evangelize the English, and settle at Newcastle—that they are under the necessity to labour for their living, and to spend much time in translating the Scriptures, and you will be able to form some idea of our case.'

CONTENTS

© Day One Publications 2005   First printed 2005

All Scripture quotations are taken from the Authorized Version

A CIP record is held at The British Library   ISBN 1 903087 76 7

ublished by Day One Publications Ryelands Road, Leominster, HR6 8NZ

01568 613 740 FAX 01568 611 473   email—sales@dayone.co.uk   www.dayone.co.uk   All rights reserved

Design and Art Direction: Steve Devane   Printed by Gutenberg, Malta

Dedication: For my girls: Rosemarie, Ellen, Bethany and Anna. Just one life to attempt great things for God

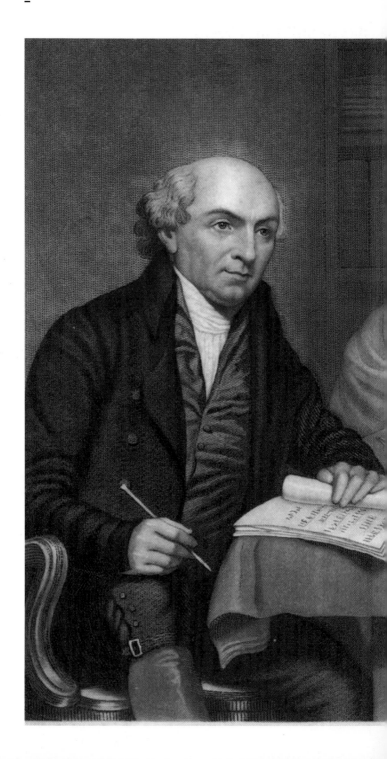

Meet William Carey

The word of God was like fire burning in William Carey's heart, continuously igniting him to challenge ungodly behaviour in both church and culture. He dared people to think biblically and rearrange their lives accordingly. He was the living, walking, talking embodiment of his own much-quoted saying: 'Expect great things from God and attempt great things for God.' Physically a small man, yet he accomplished big things for God in both England and India.

Carey used all his energy, time and gifts to bring people the Bible so that their world could be shaped by God's word. This was his vision and passion for all people throughout the whole earth. After twelve years of intense gospel work in England, he bought a one-way ticket, packed his bags, travelled 15,000 miles to India, and spent the rest of his life vigorously spreading the Bible there. In the years that followed, hundreds copied his example and became missionaries throughout the world. Arguably, William Carey had a greater influence on the development of India than anyone before or since. The impact of his life and work are still felt today in that great nation.

Carey overcame serious disease in his own life and tragedy in his family life, to play a key role in rousing the church to world mission; he has rightly been called 'the father of modern missions'. With his close friends in England he road-blocked the powerful East India Company and its total opposition to missionary work, smashed inhumane practices in India, cracked a formidable array of languages and dialects to translate the Bible, and set thousands of Indians free to understand God's truth.

Many times Carey was cast down, but he never gave up. He was a Spirit-led dynamo who wanted to make an eternal difference to people's lives: very few were the same after spending time with this energetic and radical man of vision.

1 William the Conqueror, conquered!

Take a strong-willed young boy who becomes a strong-headed teenager, put him up against a sovereign and gracious God—and watch the outcome

William Carey and his friends were up to their usual tree-climbing escapades. They had conquered most trees in the village, but there was one that proved just too difficult. William was not the kind of boy who would give up and allow a tree to beat him; he tried and tried to get to the top, until one day he fell and hurt himself badly. Sidelined by injury, the accident left him a reluctant patient in bed in his room for a few days.

Lying there, nursing his cuts and bruises; William had plenty to look at, for his room was alive with the world of nature. While still a young lad he had developed a great love for God's creation that only intensified as he grew older. He spent many happy hours rambling in Whittlebury Forest which pushed right up to the village of Paulerspury in Northamptonshire, where he was born on 17 August 1761.

William would often take his younger sister Mary and carry his younger brother Tom on his 'explorations'. Trekking the dirtiest roads and the most awkward places in these youthful expeditions, he would search for

Above: *The church font at St James the Great where William Carey was christened 23 August 1761*

Facing page: *A row of cottages in Paulerspury, the village of Carey's birth*

Above: Paulerspury, a village of around 800 people when Carey was born

fascinating wildlife: plants, shrubs, flowers, trees, butterflies, insects and birds (and their eggs). He would examine his findings with care, point out their delights and wonders, and then bring them home, catalogue them, draw them, and put them on display in his room, whether dead or alive! He gained such a knowledge of nature that they called him the 'boy-botanist.' His love of nature,

James Cook

James Cook (1728–1779) was a British explorer and navigator famous for three voyages of exploration and discovery. During his first voyage to the South Pacific as lieutenant in command of the *Endeavour*, he discovered the eastern coast of Australia, and charted its coastline along with some unknown shores of New Zealand. For his second voyage to the South Pacific he was promoted to Commander, and in 1772 set sail in the *Resolution*. Cook made the first crossing of the Antarctic Circle; found new islands and charted the New Hebrides, the volcanic islands of the Marquesas, and Easter Island. In July 1776 he set out on his third expedition, again discovering and charting new islands in the mid-Pacific in his search for a Northwest Passage between the Atlantic and Pacific oceans. In 1779 he was killed by the Hawaiian natives on the Sandwich islands.

Above: Captain James Cook, one of William's boyhood heroes

Above: Paulerspury Parish register recording the christening of William Carey, son of Edmund and Elizabeth Carey

Below: In Carey's day Whittlebury Forest and Paulerspury were joined; there is some distance between them

gardens, flowers and wildlife never left him.

Early loves

William's Uncle Peter, recently returned from Canada, may have sparked off this deep interest in nature. Peter and William hit it off instantly. Peter, a gardener with an enthusiasm for all things outdoors, spent many hours with young William pouring out thrilling stories of people from other cultures, and of new lands and languages he had come across on his travels. His life breathed adventure: he had served with General James Wolfe in Canada during the excitement when the British captured Quebec in 1759—he had so much to tell. Such an uncle ignited Carey's imagination and his uncle's interests and enthusiasms soon became William's.

Obsessed with adventure William would spend hours reading about them. He read Daniel Defoe's *Life and Adventures of Robinson Crusoe*,

but he was more interested in the real thing—fact not fiction. He devoured the *Life of Christopher Columbus* and raved on about him so much that his friends nicknamed him Columbus Carey! He lived during an age of exploration and invention, the world was opening up and many things were becoming possible. When William was nine years old Captain James Cook returned from his first South Seas voyage, and a few months later the *Northampton Mercury* announced that he would be setting off on his second voyage to make even greater discoveries. The buzz of adventurous travel set William's imagination racing to lands far away.

Nearer home William would

Top: *A cottage, dating from the same time as Carey's birthplace, can be found just down the road from Carey's first house*

Centre: *William Carey's birthplace as it was when he was born.*

Above: *The tomb of Sir Arthur and Anne Throckmorton, who recline, face to face, propped up on their elbows, smiling at each other*

Left: *The Latin inscription Carey translated when he was about twelve. It is attached to the tomb of Sir Arthur and Anne Throckmorton in the church of St James The Great, bearing witness to their loving relationship: telling us they lived together for 40 years and 17 days without a quarrel!*

often go with his friends to the old Roman road, the main link between London and Chester, and watch the various kinds of coaches rattling along, dreaming of where they had come from and where they were going to.

Languages too, fascinated him, as they would all his life. He was diligent in his Latin studies, and at the age of twelve he memorised just about all of Dyche's *Latin Vocabulary*. The day eventually came when he translated a Latin inscription near the Throckmorton's tomb in the church of St James the Great.

Hard work and learning

William was a hard working pupil. His sister Mary wrote, 'When William was in his sixth year, he discovered a great aptness for learning.' He was at an advantage when it came to education because when he was six his father was appointed schoolmaster of the village school. This gave William access to books and materials as often as he liked. His Father's new situation involved a short move from their house in Pury End to the other half of the village.

Before this move, Edmund and Elizabeth—William's parents—had been weavers working long hours from early morning to late at night, simply trying to provide the basic necessities of life. Help was at hand for Elizabeth though, as William's grandmother was living with them, and looked after William in his early years, with all the special, doting care of a grandmother in love with her first grandchild. As she entered into his world by helping him to crawl, take his first steps, and sound his

Top: The school and schoolhouse built on the same spot that Carey's family moved to when he was six

Left: The village school has spread since Carey's day. The schoolhouse where Carey lived from ages six to fourteen would have been in what is now the playground

Top: St James the Great, Paulerspury, where the young William reluctantly attended with his parents **Below:** *The plaque in the south porch*

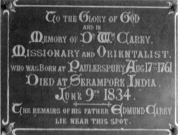

first words, it was impossible that some of her loving and gentle nature did not rub off on him.

William was persistent—very persistent. His sister Mary commented, 'Whatever he began, he finished.' This was part of Carey's nature throughout his life; he was a relentless non-quitter. In his later years he wrote, 'I can plod and persevere. This is my only genius. I can persevere in any definite pursuit. To this I owe everything.' Hence, when he recovered from his tree-fall injuries the first thing he did was to conquer the tree that had beaten him.

Yet there was one thing during those early years he had to give in to. When William left school at the age of twelve he went to work in the open air, like his Uncle Peter. He hit a major problem however, as the sun irritated the skin on his hands and face, and the pain became so bad that he couldn't even sleep at night. For two years he persevered but not even William Carey could beat the relentless rays of the sun. Yet these years were not wasted, as one of his biographers has commented: 'He learnt a mighty lesson during those two years: to plough straight you have to have your eyes firmly set on a definite mark.'

The shoemaker's apprentice

Shoemaking was becoming the chief craft of the county of Northamptonshire, promising a bright future, and after William reluctantly gave up his agricultural work, he started a seven year apprenticeship as a cordwainer. It was a skilled craft and William had to learn how to prepare the leather, cut the welts, uppers, soles and heels, sow them together and shape the shoes. He was apprenticed to Clarke Nichols of Piddington, a churchgoing man, but as Carey soon found out, a hypocrite: church on Sunday, but mean and hot tempered throughout the week.

In Nichols' home Carey shared an attic room with a fellow apprentice, John Warr, who was a real Christian with an experience of God and an understanding of that experience. At the time Carey was not at all bothered with Christianity. His mother and father attended church regularly; indeed his father was parish clerk with duties that required regular church attendance. Unwillingly William went with them to the parish church on Sundays, and half-heartedly he sat through the family Bible times throughout the week, but he had no taste for God's word. He kept the wrong kind of company in both Paulerspury and Piddington, joining in with their coarse and godless talk and becoming addicted to lying and swearing. He was far from God.

A contagious Christian

Carey had never before come across someone with a real experience of God, and he could not get away from John Warr's witness of true godliness. In the workshop during the day, and in their shared room at night, Warr's Christian witness was contagious as he talked and talked with Carey on spiritual matters. Carey liked a good argument—he hardly ever lost one—and he made sure he always had the last word.

Top: The plaque on the North wall of St. James the Great given by the Northampton Baptist Association in 1942 to commemorate the 150th year of the founding of the Baptist Missionary Society.

Above: The church of St John the Baptist in Piddington where Carey attended during the time of his resistance to God

But Warr was just as insistent, not merely wanting to win an argument, but to win a young man for Christ. He kept on, and even lent Carey books to read. Warr had a life to match his words, and he amazingly managed to get William to attend some prayer meetings at his church in Hackleton. God was at work and Carey was softening; he had never been to a prayer meeting where people were serious with God and fervent about the condition of their souls. This was something totally new, something worth thinking about.

God used the things Carey was interested in to create in him an interest in higher things. On Clarke Nichols' bookshelves Carey spotted a Greek New Testament. His love of languages surfaced and he wanted to learn Greek! He knew a man in Paulerspury who could help him, and so he started reading the New Testament in its original language; at the same time adding a second language to his learning.

The overwhelming force of truth was getting through to Carey; he knew he had to do something about it. Self-sufficient and proud, he tried to heal his own soul. He determined to use

Above: The first panel of six from the William Carey Mural in Carey Baptist Church, Moulton, Northampton. It includes Carey's home and church in Paulerspury

his will-power to stop his lying and swearing, and he even began praying. He became religious and started going to his parish church three times on a Sunday. But it was no good. He could not get any peace for his conscience or any reality in his religion.

Matters came to a head over the Christmas of 1777. With his Christmas box money in his pocket he went to Northampton to buy treats for himself. Nichols had also given him some money to buy a few things that he himself wanted. As William was about to pay for his own things he found he had overspent by a shilling. Now he had a crafty idea. The

Carey's brother and sisters

Carey's youngest sister Mary, had a spinal disease which left her paralysed by the age of 25; for the next 50 years her suffering was very great and she was confined to bed. Yet she did not become bitter, but remained a 'sweet tempered, self sacrificing humble Christian lady who thought more of others than of herself.' She was zealous for God and faithful in praying for William; in her room she ran a Bible class for children, and though it caused her pain, yet she used her only moveable limb, her right arm, to write on a slate to teach. During the years William was in India she wrote him many long letters giving him all the news from home. Her pastor said, 'Her work in affliction, in its way, was as great as that which her great brother wrought.'

Carey's younger sister, Ann, married a farmer who opened up his home for gospel preaching. Ann took Mary to live with her and spent much of her time mothering her.

His younger brother Tom became a soldier but retired from the army when he was wounded. In 1793 William visited him in Bradford and found him worshipping the Lord. One of his children, Eustace, would later join William in India as a missionary.

The Angus Library at Regents Park College, Oxford, holds letters from William Carey to both his sisters and a few from them to him. These can only be seen under certain criteria; please visit for details: www.lib.ox.ac.uk/libraries/guides/REG.html

Above: From St James the Great looking towards Carey's birthplace

ironmonger had given Carey a counterfeit shilling as his Christmas gift, so Carey decided to switch it for a genuine shilling from the money his master had given him. He would put the dud coin in the change that he would give back to his master and insist it belonged to him. Inventive plan, but God exposed it and his master found out! Carey was ashamed of his dishonesty and thought everyone in the village knew; he was so fearful that he refused to go out—and he began to pray seriously. He says, 'I at this time sought the Lord perhaps much more earnestly than ever; but with shame and fear.'

God's Spirit was leading Carey towards the Saviour, and though he could never put a precise date on his conversion, somewhere between the ages of seventeen and eighteen he eventually gave in to Christ as his Lord and Saviour. Normally Carey never gave in— but he learnt that no-one fights God and wins. He had been conquered; he had to bow his knee; he could not have the last word this time. William Carey submitted his life to God and he found peace and the meaning of life. Nothing would ever be the same again.

Telling others

Carey soon realised the gospel was not just true for him, it was true for others also, and they needed to hear it. He became a fervent evangelist having a real longing for people to come to know Christ as he himself did. Back home in Paulerspury his family were

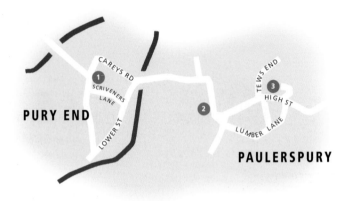

KEY TO PLACES

1 CAREY'S BIRTHPLACE   2 ST JAMES THE GREAT CHURCH   3 THE SCHOOLHOUSE

Above: The cairn marking the place of William Carey's birthplace made from the same stone that formed his cottage

amazed at the change in him, and at first they did not like it. Whenever he visited home he was on a mission to bring his parents to God: he burned the playing cards, took over the family Bible time, led prayers, and was insistent in urging them to turn to God. His sister Mary later wrote, 'I often wished he would not bring his religion home. He asked leave to pray in the family. He always mentioned the words— "all our righteousnesses are as filthy rags." That used to touch my pride and raise my indignation.' But eventually, through his consistent witness both his sisters, Mary and Ann, came to Christ and were baptised in the River Tove by 1783. His sisters' stories became moving examples of faithfulness and devotion to God and to one another.

This early passion of William to make Christ known to those who did not yet know him, would find massive expression in his later years. His life had been changed and he had to tell others what the Saviour had done for him. Carey just could not keep quiet. The future direction of his life was set.

Above: The hill Carey walked up to go to church

TRAVEL INFORMATION

Paulerspury

Take junction 15A off the M1 and join the A43 to Towcester. At Towcester join the A5 south and travel approximately 2.5 miles (4 km) before turning right into Paulerspury.

This delightfully quiet cottage village is named after the Lord of the Manor, Sir Robert de Pavely (d. 1346) and a pear orchard (Perey). Pavelis' Perey soon became Paulerspury.

William Carey was born in the part of the village called 'Pury End'. Walk down 'Carey's Road', and you can see the two new (private) houses standing where his parents' cottage once stood. From these houses go back towards St James the Great and walk up the grass hill to the church. This was the hill Carey used to walk up as a lad.

St James the Great church dates back to the 12th Century. Here William was christened on 23 August 1761, and here his father Edmund was parish clerk. See Edmund's grave just outside the south porch.

The village school now covers the ground in which Carey used to live with his parents in their school house.

An initiative called 'The Carey Experience' has been set up which is a 'trail of five churches connected with the life and work of William Carey.' See their website www.thecareyexperience.co.uk

Margaret Williams is acting as coordinator, you may phone her if you wish to gain access to St James the Great church.
(☎ 01604 719187)

Above: The tomb of Sir Robert de Pavely, after whom Paulerspury is named

② Ignited by Cook

William Carey began to bring his powerful mind captive to God's word. This enabled him to persevere during the most severe trials, and led him to begin dreaming big dreams for God

Having found new life in Christ, Carey now had some big issues to think through. He began to engage his still youthful, yet rigorous and well-ordered, mind to sorting out some of the implications of his new life. Which church should he join? He had been attending the prayer meetings at Hackleton during the week, but the parish church on Sundays. He found more spiritual help from the Dissenters (a title for any Protestant group not in the Church of England) but they were at that time belittled, counted as socially inferior to Anglicans, and discriminated against. To join them would damage his social standing. He also felt some loyalty to the Church of England as both his grandfather and his father had been parish clerks. To which community of believers should he belong? It was not an easy decision.

Carey made his choice on Sunday 10 February 1779. King George III proclaimed this day as a day of national fasting and prayer because of the bad turn of events for the British in the

Above: The second panel in Moulton's Mural depicting Carey as Cobbler and Teacher and showing the Moulton cottage—Teaching—Shoe-making and repairs—Nichols' cottage interior

Facing page: St John the Baptist church, Piddington, where Dorothy Plackett was christened on 25 January 1756, and where she later married William Carey in June 1781

Top: Carey Baptist Church, Hackleton which stands behind the site of the Meeting house where Carey worshipped

Above: The Hackleton meeting house as it was in Carey's day

American War of Independence. Carey decided to go to Hackleton for this day, and heard the preacher, Thomas Chater, spell out the cost of discipleship. At some point in the sermon he used Hebrews 13:13 to urge his hearers to abandon themselves to Christ completely and to follow him. The sermon pierced Carey's soul and he decided that for him the reproach of the cross meant joining the 'despised dissenters'. From this decision of joining nonconformity he never turned back, and typically went as far as he could in his commitment, adding his name near the top of the list when Hackleton Dissenting Church was formed on 19 May 1781.

Anxiety over Assurance

Carey's mind was fertile, he was only in his late teens and he wanted to know as much as he possibly could about his faith. He devoured Christian books and studied the Bible intently. His workshop was dubbed 'Carey's College' as he discussed his studies with colleagues and customers alike. In his ever deepening search for spiritual understanding he came across a group of mystics who lived a short distance away in Quinton. The leader of this group was as determined and strong minded as William, and for a while Carey had met his match. Sadly, this leader succeeded in convincing Carey that 'he was far short of

real spiritual light and feeling,' and Carey was thrown into three horrible years of wondering if he was truly a believer; he was filled with anxiety over his spiritual state, lacking assurance of his faith. Carey needed spiritual help and God graciously provided it from two sources.

In September 1779 Carey's boss Clarke Nichols died and his business was taken over by Thomas Old, a godly man. Carey enjoyed working for him and benefited from the regular visits of Thomas Scott, a young Anglican clergyman from Weston Underwood in Buckinghamshire. Scott knew the value of personal help during a time of spiritual crisis, for he himself had received such from John Newton of Olney. Scott gave Carey some invaluable one-to-one sessions and Carey began to attend his preaching. Carey owed so much to Scott and he never forgot it. Forty years later William wrote, 'If there be anything of the work of God in my soul, I owe much of it to Mr Scott's preaching, when I first set out in the ways of the Lord.'

Carey was also strengthened by a book aptly named *A Help to Zion's Travellers*, by Robert Hall. William was disappointed with the Hackleton fellowship, who instead of gathering around to

Above, left: Thomas Old's workshop has now been replaced by modern buildings in the Jetty, very near to Carey Baptist Church

Above, right: Thomas Scott, a curate at Weston Underwood and Olney before becoming Rector of Aston Sanford in 1801

help him, gave body language signs that spoke of distance and disapproval because he mixed with the mystics. He occasionally began to go elsewhere for Bible teaching, and came across Thomas Skinner, pastor of the Baptist meeting in Towcester, who introduced Carey to Robert Hall's book. Carey just could not put it down. Published in 1781, it addressed hot theological issues of the day and Carey read it with 'rapture; and drank it eagerly to the bottom of the cup' finding it to be as the 'sweetest wine.' It was just the book the 20–year old Carey needed. Having been looking into his own heart for months and months to see if he really did have feelings for Christ, this book told him to look out to Christ and to trust him. With its message of salvation to all who believed, it gave Carey confidence and assurance of salvation. The book formed a defining moment in his life and it never left Carey's side; he even took it to India with him and it was found amongst his personal possessions after his death. By 1783 Carey was through his doubts and had assurance of his faith in Christ.

Two public pledges

Thomas Scott was not the only frequent visitor to Carey's workshop. A certain Miss Dorothy Plackett, Thomas Old's sister-in-law, also dropped by a few times. Carey knew her from the Hackleton church for she was a daughter of one of its leaders. She was five years older than William, but a relationship started up between them. What did they see in each other? It certainly was

Pictured: Carey's copy of A Help to Zion's Travellers, found in his personal property in India after he died. Carey's neat notes can be clearly seen on the pages. They form a kind of index to the contents of the book. Most of them are on the left hand page, written sideways, for easy reference when thumbing back. This copy is now in the Library of the Bristol Baptist College

Above: William and Dorothy's home in Piddington as it was then—part of a row of cottages. A modern private residence is now on this site

not educational equality for Dorothy was illiterate as there was no school in the village. Was it spiritual kinship? She certainly had a love for God and an almost puritanical upbringing, and maybe her love for Christ met Carey's love for Christ. Whatever the attraction, things moved quickly and they publicly declared their love for each other in marriage at Piddington Church on Sunday 10 June 1781. William was not quite 20 and Dorothy was 25. The special promises of loving each other 'for better or worse, for richer or poorer, in sickness and in health' that William and Dorothy made that day would be tested to the full in the rollercoaster years that lay ahead.

They set up home in Hackleton, before moving very soon to a small cottage in Piddington. Here Carey kept the little garden looking good, continued his shoemaking work, devoted time to his Greek and Latin language studies, whilst also pursuing his scripture studies. After a year or so their first daughter was born. They named her Ann, after William's grandmother who had so 'especially' cared for William during his toddling days. Their new baby brought them sleepless nights, but also great joy as they lived happily together.

Neither marriage nor a new baby distracted Carey from his ardent pursuit of Christian knowledge and obedience. Still he read and studied as widely and deeply as he could. The whole issue of Christian baptism was now before him: perhaps he had been wondering what to do for baby Ann? On one occasion he heard a sermon from a paedo-baptist (a believer in infant baptism), which drove him to check out the New Testament on the subject of baptism. After his usual thorough study he reached the conclusion that baptism was for those 'of conscious faith and consecration.' So he decided to be baptised, and at six in the morning of 5 October 1783 he went into the waters of the River Nene in Northampton where John Ryland Jr, co-pastor of College Lane Baptist church, baptised him. There were not many witnesses present that morning, yet a pledge to follow Jesus was publicly made.

Carey begins to preach

Through his Bible studies William grew strong in his understanding of the Christian faith and it was not long before he began speaking in public at the Hackleton 'Sabbath evening conferences'. His preaching went down well, indeed so well that when he finished people clapped! This did not help Carey much in his lifelong fight with pride, so he tried to dismiss the applause by putting it down to the ignorance of the people.

By June 1782, he was also preaching at Earls Barton Baptist Church. After his first visit he found himself ministering there every fortnight for three and a half years. The 21 year old Carey delighted in serving the Lord in this way, and spent many happy

Above: The Place of Carey's early morning baptism in the River Nene in 1783

Above, left: The Earls Barton Baptist Church where Carey preached fortnightly for three and a half years. Right:The pulpit from which Carey used to preach at Hackleton

hours in sermon preparation. He used the six mile walk to Earls Barton to admire God's creation in the beautiful Northamptonshire countryside, as well as to meditate on the fuller revelation in the Scriptures as his mind scrolled through the sermon he was about to deliver. Over the years he came to know this church well and enjoyed their fellowship, though he was often grieved by some of the petty divisions he found among them.

The worst of times

Sometime in 1783 William and his infant daughter Ann, contracted a severe fever. It affected him so badly that he began to lose his hair. He remedied this by going to William Wilson of Olney, a hairdresser and wig-maker—though not a very good wig-maker—and purchased a rather ill-fitting wig. Carey became desperately ill, but he fought it and eventually after eighteen months, recovered. However, poor little Ann did not, and tragically, after struggling for her life she died before her second birthday. William and Dorothy's grief was immense. The chatter of infant lips and the padding of tiny feet would no longer be heard in their empty cottage. Many, many tears were shed over the next months by these grieving young parents.

On 31 December 1783 death visited the Carey family again. Thomas Old, William's brother-in-law and employer, died unexpectedly. William took over his business as well as the care of his wife and their children. These were desperate times as William was already struggling financially.

Top: Moulton Village sign depicting Carey as very much part of its history

Above: The South Sea Islands which Cook discovered and for which Carey prayed

The winter of 1784 was severe and William had to trudge through snow and cold seeking orders and fetching payment. He wore himself out trying to make ends meet; he extended the business from making new shoes to buying and selling second hand shoes. He even started up an evening school for the village children to provide more income for his widened family. Yet times were hard and money was scarce. They were difficult days.

Always adventurous

In the middle of William's grief and troubles, he began to read the accounts of Captain Cook's last voyage. Cook was a boyhood hero, and now, some ten years later, William could read the accounts of his travels first hand. Here were inspiring stories of the people Captain Cook met and the places he came across. Carey found the books to be thrilling; they appealed to his sense of adventure and gripped his mind.

God used these books to touch Carey's heart. He read them with a spiritual mind and saw beyond the adventure of discovery to the need of the people in the South Sea Islands. Here were people living without Christ—and the account of their behaviour and customs proved it. They were in darkness and would die in darkness, and be in darkness for ever, unless someone told them about the salvation that can be found in Christ. Years later Carey wrote, 'Reading Cook's voyages was the first thing that turned my mind to think of missions.' Zeal to reach these people with the gospel began to course through his veins, burning his heart, and thrilling his mind. He began to

Left: Carey's Moulton cottage where he and Dorothy settled in 1785. His church is alongside

Below: The plaque on the wall of Carey's Moulton cottage

have a vision—a *big* vision that one day servants of Christ would take the gospel to these islands; it is said, that from this time on 'Nobody ever heard him pray without making intercession for Cook's islands.'

Rebuilding their lives

At the beginning of 1785 William and Dorothy were trying to rebuild their lives after all the illnesses, poverty and tragedy of the past eighteen months. An opportunity arose to move to Moulton and start a village school, whilst at the same time continuing shoemaking. This would give them a new start, as well as some much-needed extra income. So on 25 March, William and Dorothy left Piddington with all its mixed blessings and moved to Moulton, four miles (6km) north-east of Northampton.

They moved into a cottage, built for a shoemaker, and began making it home. It soon became a full house as Felix was born in October 1786, followed two years later by another son, William. In 1789 Peter, named no doubt after his great-uncle, was born and added to the noise and happiness of the home. Outside the cottage, his sons would have toddled or crawled watching their father enjoying himself clearing the ground, planting seeds and bulbs, to create an attractive and economically useful garden.

A multi-tasking man

Carey, unafraid of hard work, wanted to do the best he possibly could at all he did. He was keenly aware that to properly teach the children in his school, he himself needed to grow in knowledge. So, he continued with his disciplined reading and studying. He learnt to

Above: The original water trough in Carey's Moulton cottage where he used to soak his leather

lessons from his heart, longing that his pupils might feel these subjects, and not just learn the facts. But it was Carey's geography lessons that came alive with the passion of a man who was gripped by the need of the nations. His visual aids were stunning. He gathered sheets of paper, pasted them together with his shoe-maker's wax and made a map of the world, which he hung on his wall. On the nations he would put whatever data he could find about them. He managed to lay his hands on Guthrie's *Geographical Grammar,* John Entick's *The Present State of the British Empire* and he read the international news section of the weekly newspaper the *Northampton Mercury.* Whenever he came across new information on any nation he would transfer it to his wall map. He was almost obsessed with finding these facts. In addition to the map, he used his leather working skills to craft a leather globe.

Through these media Carey would teach, and his fervour often took over as he pointed to the nations and said to the class: 'And these are pagans, pagans!' for to him they were not just statistics, they were real people with real souls who needed spiritual help. The desire to reach these nations for Christ burned bright in his heart. It would one day result in him teaching a school in a very different part of the world.

multi-task: reading from a book perched on the bench while he cobbled shoes. He majored in his preferences of language and geography and even developed some knowledge of Hebrew, Italian, French, and Dutch. His ability to learn languages gained him a reputation, and one of his employers, the far-sighted Thomas Gotch, a business entrepreneur and young deacon of Andrew Fuller's church in Kettering, offered him ten shillings a fortnight to continue in his language studies, thus freeing up time from his shoemaking.

Carey's school reflected Carey's interests. He loved history, travel and science, and taught these

HACKLETON

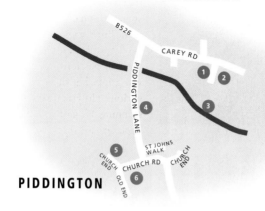

BS26
CAREY RD
PIDDINGTON LANE
ST JOHNS WALK
CHURCH END
CHURCH RD
CHURCH END
OLD END

PIDDINGTON

KEY TO PLACES

1 CAREY BAPTIST CHURCH

2 THE JETTY, WHERE THOMAS OLD OWNED A WORKSHOP

3 THE BROOK FOR BAPTISMS

4 CAREY'S COTTAGE

5 ST JOHN THE BAPTIST WHERE WILLIAM AND DOROTHY MARRIED

6 THE WORKSHOP OF CLARKE NICHOLS

TRAVEL INFORMATION

Piddington and Hackleton are within walking distance of each other. It is best to park near Carey Church in Hackleton, and then walk down The Jetty and across the field to Piddington. Reach Hackleton by exiting the M1 at Junction 15 and joining the A508 towards Northampton. Take the B256 and drive approximately 3 miles (5km) to Hackleton.

Piddington

Piddington is a very friendly village full of helpful people. Here you can see 21 Church Road, a privately owned house, but this was the site of Clarke Nichols' workshop. You can also see the 12th century Church of St John the Baptist where William attended three times each Sunday when he was under conviction of sin, and where he and Dorothy were married. In Piddington Lane you can find a cream washed cottage on the site of Carey's old cottage. It was here that William and Dorothy set up home for two years. It may have been on this site that Dorothy returned from Leicester and in this place that John Thomas (see chapter 5) eventually persuaded her to go to India.

Hackleton

Here you see The Jetty—a row of four terraced cottages. In one of the upper ones Thomas Old had his workshop. The Carey Baptist church was built in front of the old Hackleton Meeting House in 1889. If you wish to gain access to Carey Baptist church please phone 'The Carey Experience' coordinator, Margaret Williams ☎ 01604 719187.

❸ Disturbing the dinosaurs

Carey was mission through and through. If you could have cut him open you would have found mission tattooed on his inside. Whether he was teaching school, cobbling shoes, preaching sermons or talking with friends, his subject was invariably mission

The move to Moulton brought with it a move in church. William was still preaching fortnightly at Earls Barton, but on the other Sundays he and Dorothy began attending the Baptist Church in Moulton, where they were warmly welcomed. This was a church with a good though short history, but a present crisis. It was now dwindling in numbers and frequently having to cancel its services. The building reflected the people—run down. But Carey began to encourage them and preach for them on his free Sundays. God used his preaching to renew the small church and to bring people to salvation. Within a matter of months they began to pressure him to become their pastor, just as the Earls Barton group were doing.

In demand

Carey sought advice about these pressures from John Sutcliff, the pastor of Olney Baptist Church. William had become a member of Olney in July 1785, only a few

Above: Panel three of the Moulton Mural depicting Carey's preaching and study. Here are scenes of Carey's baptism—Widow Wallis' house—Hackleton and Olney meeting houses—Moulton Baptist Church

Facing page: Moulton cottages

Top: *Olney Baptist Church where Carey preached for commendation to the ministry in 1785*

Centre: *The entrance to William and Dorothy's cottage in Moulton*

Above: *Carey Baptist Church, Moulton*

months after moving to Moulton. Sutcliff encouraged Carey to preach to the Olney Church later that same July so they could test him for the work of the ministry. It was an awesome experience for Carey. The building was by far the biggest he had ever preached in, seating 700 people. The people themselves were dogmatic in their beliefs and had a reputation for being fond of a doctrinal ministry. They had given their pastors hard times over very small matters. The day came when Carey stood in the pulpit along the north wall gazing out over the box pews and 'cumbrous galleries' which hung from the other three walls. It was overwhelming for him and he made a complete mess of the sermon. Nerves? Inexperience? Whatever, the Olney Baptists did not think they could commend him for the ministry, but they advised him to come back and preach again another time 'in order that further trial may be made of his ministerial gifts.'

The next summer, 1786, Carey was back, preaching at Olney again for the same purpose. The word 'failure' was not in his vocabulary. This time the church gave him their warm approval and commissioned him: 'To preach the gospel, wherever God in his providence might call him,' which for now meant Moulton. So, to his already heavy workload of school teaching and shoe making, William added the responsibilities of what he called 'the highest

Above: A thatched house in Moulton dating to 1695

honour on earth'—the pastoral office.

The day of William's ordination was set for Wednesday 1 August 1787. He would celebrate his twenty-sixth birthday in two weeks time. Moulton was buzzing and the church was packed. Among the men taking part in the service were John Ryland who led, John Sutcliff who preached from 2 Timothy 4:5, and Andrew Fuller who gave the charge to the church. These men, together with Carey, in a matter of a few years would change the face of the English Baptist scene, and in a few more years, the face of world mission. They struck up a warm and close fellowship.

Carey threw himself into the work of the ministry with all the Carey-thoroughness that was possible. He did not want to miss a moment. On 13 October 1787 he wrote to his father, 'How important is time. One moment gone is gone eternally, the opportunity to honour God, or benefit our fellow mortals, irrevocably past.' He was faithful and zealous in his regular preaching of God's word, and he even had the thrill of baptising his own wife Dorothy in October 1787. William was a brave pastor who did not shun from exercising discipline on unrepentant rebellious church members, but he was a loving pastor who moved among his people when smallpox struck the village in 1788. He was zealous in gospel preaching and saw real conversions which lasted, and became his 'joy and crown'. The number of people attending

Left: Interior of Carey Baptist Church, Moulton, today

the church increased so much that there was not enough room to contain them, so they began a new building project. In order to build these people into a dynamic church, Carey established a covenant which bound the members together and kept them on the same track. The church became a good and happy place to be, as the secretary recorded: (in his spelling) 'Whe met in peas and parted in younity.'

World vision increases

The group of friends Carey now mixed with fuelled his gospel missionary vision. In their own way each had begun to make a dent in the hyper-Calvinism that

Hyper-Calvinism

John Calvin (1509–1564), taught and preached powerfully in Geneva, Switzerland. His *Institutes of the Christian Religion* are amongst the most influential of Christian theologies ever to have been written. They stress the glory and the sovereignty of God in all things. A hundred years or so after Calvin, many Baptists continued to follow some of his teachings and became known as Calvinistic Baptists. From this group came Baptists who maximised his teaching on the sovereignty of God and ended up minimizing the responsibility of human beings. These were the hyper-Calvinists who would not offer the gospel freely and openly to their hearers nor plead with them to embrace Christ for salvation, and ended up simply declaring that sinners are doomed. C.H. Spurgeon commented that this system of theology 'chilled many Churches to their very soul.' It also killed evangelism and missionary work.

Above, left: Carey's Moulton Pulpit from where he zealously explained God's word—now to be seen in the Carey Museum

Above, right: The plaque on the wall of Carey Baptist Church, Moulton, marking the spot where where Carey's pulpit used to be

gripped their churches.

Andrew Fuller, pastor of Gold Street Baptist Church, Kettering, whom Spurgeon called, 'The greatest theologian of the nineteenth century', had seen the weakness of hyper-calvinism, and in 1785 published *The Gospel Worthy of All Acceptation* stating clearly that the gospel is to be preached to all and that it is the duty of all who hear it to put their faith in Christ. John Ryland, pastor of College Lane Baptist Church in Northampton, lived in the shadow of his forceful, and sometimes eccentric father, John C Ryland, and yet took off his father's hyper-Calvinist strait-jacket with the help of John Newton of Olney. John Sutcliff was the cautious and patient pastor of Olney Baptist Church; he initiated the call to prayer for the Northampton Association in 1784, in which churches of all kinds were urged to join in earnest and united prayer that God would pour out his Spirit upon ministers and churches in every place. Many churches responded positively and by the summer of 1784 were meeting once a month especially to pray for revival. It was a serious call with a serious response.

Into this group of zealous, spiritually hot men, came Carey who turned the temperature up a

Above: The old 'sheep dip'—the probable place of Dorothy's baptism a few hundred yards behind the chapel *Below:* Andrew Fuller of Kettering

few degrees. They soon became 'one heart and one soul' in their lives, prayers and longings. They preached in each other's churches and fired each other to serve God better. They read the same authors, especially the works coming from the New England pastor Jonathan Edwards. They would meet together as a foursome to pray, to read, to fast, and to encourage each other in their longing for God to work in their land as well as in distant lands. On 21 January 1788 Ryland wrote in his journal: 'Brethren Fuller, Sutcliff, Carey, and I, kept this day as a private fast in my study... our chief design was to implore a revival of godliness in our own souls, in our Churches, and in the Church at large.' These four pastors studied and discussed the Scriptures together, especially passages in the Old Testament prophets which spoke of the glory of God's kingdom in future ages.

Carey looked on the Bible as 'the progressive unfolding of God's world-missionary purpose.' He studied the Old Testament, which he considered missionary prophecy; and he studied the New Testament, which he saw full of missionary exploits and achievements. He became consumed with the urgency of taking the gospel to the lost. He knew people were praying, which

Above: Carey Baptist Church, Moulton Below: John Ryland Jr of Northampton

he joined in with, but, he argued: do not just pray something—do something! Carey became convinced that God would work in the nations by actually using people to *go* to those nations and preach. Carey shared his ideas and thoughts with his three close friends, and they talked endlessly about them.

'Out of the overflow of the heart the mouth speaks'

The day came when Carey had the chance to give his views a wider hearing. He was at a minister's fraternal in Northampton, which the elder John C Ryland was chairing. Carey had the opportunity of raising a question for discussion and it was obvious what he would ask. He had been thinking about it, preaching on it, praying about it and discussing this subject for years; it was scorching his heart. He chose his words carefully and asked clearly:

'Whether the command given to the apostles to teach all nations was not obligatory on all succeeding ministers to the end of the world, seeing that the accompanying promise was of equal extent.' It was such a provocative question. His friends could not believe he had the nerve to ask it. The 'aged and respectable' men in the meeting almost had apoplexy! Carey was disturbing a classroom of theological dinosaurs. And, though his son later disputed it, yet John Ryland senior gave what Carey called, an 'abashing rebuke'. He fixed his eyes on Carey, frowned, and with some vehemence said something like: 'Young man, sit down, sit down! You're an enthusiast. When God pleases to convert the heathen, He'll do it without consulting you and me.' The words were chosen to shut Carey up. The word 'enthusiast' in those days was a theological insult given to any religious person who claimed intimacy with God and who took the gospel out of the four walls of a church building; it was the abusive word used to discredit the early Methodists. Moreover, the words 'young man' were a put-down to Carey's inexperience.

The question was not discussed and the meeting moved on to something safer; but the irrepressible Carey would not be silenced by the prejudice and error of older men. His vision was massive: for ministers of the gospel to go to pagans of different cultures and languages in lands and islands thousands of miles away to preach the gospel. He was intent on fulfilling this dream and he took every opportunity to speak of his vision. His preaching became more and more challenging and direct, as he not only pleaded with the lost to come to Christ, but also urged Christians to reach the lost. Some said they could smell heresy in his preaching. When he preached at College Lane in Northampton some of the members would not even attend!

Carey began one-to-one vision casting, speaking with his fellow ministers, trying to get them to own his vision. He appealed to their prayer purpose of 1784 and

Above: Moulton has been the winner of Britain's Best Kept Village award

Above: The stained glass window at Moulton Baptist Church, bearing the inscription, 'Expect great things from God, attempt great things for God'

reasoned that to pray for the spread of the gospel was great, but why not also get up and go—obey the Lord's commission in Matthew 28:19 and 'enable God to respect and answer their pleadings.' But it proved hard work. The older ministers thought he had a wild and impractical scheme in his head, and even Fuller, one of his best friends commented, 'If the Lord should make windows in heaven, could such a thing be?' (2 Kings 7:2). Some objected that the Lord's commission only applied to the first apostles. 'If that were so,' Carey responded 'then we must limit the command to baptise and the promise of the Lord's presence to them too!' Others said it was impossible to go to heathen lands because there were far too many difficulties. But Carey pointed to the work of English traders in foreign lands—just in order to make money! Some said the time had not yet come to go and preach to the heathen, so Carey told them to stop praying for them! Still others agued that there was far too much to do in England without going abroad. Carey agreed on the need in England—but reasoned there was far more to do abroad where people did not even have a Bible in their own language! Carey had an answer for every objection; he would not give up.

The idea of a booklet

Very little headway seemed to be made with all this vision casting, but in God's providence Carey met a man who had an idea to take the vision forward. In 1788 Carey was in Birmingham raising money to rebuild the chapel at Moulton, when he met Thomas Potts, a deacon of Cannon Street Baptist Church. Potts was 'an adventurous young merchant-businessman-trader' and the two men immediately hit it off. They were soon in deep discussion about Carey's vision for world mission. Potts urged Carey to write a book 'to inform and arouse the Churches' of this great need; even promising generous financial assistance towards the cost.

It was a great idea, and though Carey knew it must be done, yet he did not feel able to write the book. He tried to persuade his friends, Ryland, Sutcliff and Fuller to write it, but they declined, and urged him to go

ahead, and they would offer their help in advising and revising. Potts had said to Carey: 'If you can't do it [write it] as you wish, do it as you can.' So Carey, with all his other responsibilities of husband, father, pastor, school teacher, and shoe maker, now faced up to the task of writing a book that would be the hard copy of his own heart and mind—a book into which he would pour his soul and which aimed to move British Baptists to missionary work.

The move to Leicester

Village life could only hold a man with a mind like Carey's for so long. Inquisitive, exploratory, and adventurous with a big outlook, he was far from having a village mentality. So in February 1789, when Harvey Lane Baptist Church in Leicester, approached him to be their probationary pastor, he felt a strong pull.

Not that he was unhappy at Moulton. On the contrary, over the past few years he had seen the church grow as God used his ministry to win the lost and build up Christians. He had a strong bond with his people and he knew God's blessing on his ministry. A pastor does not easily walk away from a work God has so used him in, or from a people he is so deeply attached to. And yet Carey could not get Leicester out of his mind. He spent five weeks praying, considering, and asking his friends and family whether he should stay or go. He was open

Above and facing page: *Scenes from Moulton, a beautiful well-kept village that Carey found hard to leave*

and honest with the fellowship at Moulton, and on 2 April he told them about it, asking for their prayers. They immediately began to meet every Monday to pray for themselves and their pastor in this situation. A month later he accepted the call to Leicester.

What made him accept? It was not the extra money he would get in Leicester because his stipend only increased a little to £40 a year; even in Leicester he had to supplement his income by school teaching and shoe-making. And it was not because Harvey Lane was 'a better church' than Moulton. Harvey Lane had been through some major problems of disunity and strife, and recently some of its members had to be disciplined for unbiblical behaviour. They had gone through pastors like a child gets through sweets. He was going to take on a difficult situation.

What then made him accept? Opportunity. Leicester's population growth was phenomenal, nearly tripling in size from the beginning of the century. There were around 13,000 people living within its boundaries. A publication from earlier that century described Leicester as a 'large and populous old town with a great many good buildings.' There would be so many people to reach! And in Leicester there would be opportunities for influence that he simply would not have if he stayed in Moulton. Carey thrived on challenge and he loved adventure. He did not want to live at a standstill so he thought the upheaval of moving family and saying goodbye to so many close friends worthwhile, because of the big opportunities Leicester offered to serve God.

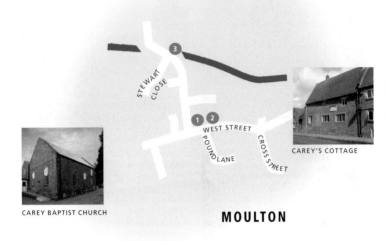

CAREY'S COTTAGE

CAREY BAPTIST CHURCH

MOULTON

KEY TO PLACES

1 CAREY BAPTIST CHURCH
2 CAREY'S COTTAGE—NOW HOUSING A SMALL MUSEUM
3 POSSIBLE PLACE OF DOROTHY'S BAPTISM

Above: *Cottages in Moulton*

TRAVEL INFORMATION

Moulton

Leave M1 at Junction 15 and join the A508 towards Northampton. Follow this as it becomes the A45 until you come to the junction with the A43. Take the A43 towards Kettering, continuing over a major roundabout until you see a sign to Moulton. Turn left along Ashley Lane and enter Moulton, a beautifully kept and attractive ancient village. A Baptist builder from last century ensured that some

Above: Carey Baptist Church, Moulton, this was The Moulton Baptist meeting house where William became Pastor in 1787

of the street names in the village were named in relation to Carey (Carey Close, Fuller Road, Ryland Road, Greenwood Close, Harvey Lane).

Here you will find Carey Baptist Church, which was where Carey ministered. Inside the church you can see the memorial tablet standing above the place where Carey had his pulpit. Be sure also to inspect the fascinating Mural on the wall, which tells the story of Carey in six panels. It was unveiled on 29 November 1991, and was designed and painted by Stella Kettle and colleagues of the Moulton Art Group.

Notice the stained glass window in the porch dedicated on 27 October 1996. The cross surmounts the globe on an open Bible. India is prominent on the globe. The pewter lettering tells of Carey's famous statement. The combination of stained glass and pewter in this window is unique.

Here you can see Carey's cottage, which once stood in a row, but was preserved when the others were demolished. Part of the cottage houses a small but interesting museum where you can see many items related to Carey, his work and ministry. Arrange access once again by contacting the ever helpful Margaret Williams ☎ 01604 719187.

4 Setting ice on fire

Nottingham and Kettering! Small places in the world's eyes, but during a seismic four months in 1792 all heaven was watching the unfolding events that would result in immeasurable benefit for the world

Once in Leicester, Carey made the most of his new opportunities. He joined the nonconformist committee and soon bonded with its chairman, Dr Thomas Arnold, and its treasurer, Robert Brewin. All three men had a spiritual concern for humanity, and a longing to do all they could to better peoples lives. Together they made a formidable group as they rolled up their sleeves in the cause of justice, righteousness and truth. They called attention to the plight of prisoners who were badly treated, and mentally ill patients who were misunderstood and abused. They spoke out against the slave trade—with Carey frequently praying publicly for the slaves. These men spent time together sharing common interests, and Carey lost himself in their libraries. In Brewin he found another lover of nature and frequently browsed his 'extensive garden with rare plants, pomegranates and prize auriculas.'

Carey's probing mind brought him into contact with the young Leicester radical Richard Phillips.

Above: *Thomas Paine, 1737–1809 an English radical thinker and writer who emigrated to America and actively supported American independence from England*

Facing page: *Images from Leicester Diwali festival. Carey would not have to go so far today in order to meet his Indian friends*

The year Carey and his family moved to Leicester, 1789, the French revolution was just beginning, reviving memories of the American Revolution; the political radicalism of these movements was felt in England—and it had many followers. Carey was in sympathy with republican ideals, but Richard Phillips wholeheartedly embraced them. Phillips started *The Leicester Herald* in 1792, and used this newspaper for his outspoken views; he founded a Philosophical Institute which became a hotbed of ideas as he arranged for lectures from likeminded radicals. The town's authorities were twitchy and eventually imprisoned Phillips in 1793 for selling Thomas Paine's book *The Rights Of Man*. That Carey should be found in such company says a lot about his own radical thinking and his intellectual ability. One can only imagine the Christian contributions Carey made to the debates and discussions in these circles, as he sought to bring the force of God's truth into every area of life.

Church and family

Yet it was church work that occupied Carey more than anything else. He began as probationary pastor on 22 June 1789 and the first few months went well. The 60 people in membership appreciated his ministry, numbers grew, and the church added a front gallery in February 1790. All seemed good and set for growth and expansion; then the devil went to work and tried to ruin what God was sowing. A few members fell into open sin, and the remaining demanded that something be done. The church became divided: 'bitter strife made havoc, the fellowship was shattered.' The growth stopped and misery took the place of joy. Carey bared his heart to Fuller saying, 'He was distressed beyond measure at the

Left: Thomas Paine's book 'The Rights Of Man'. George Monbiot, a British newspaper columnist and academic says of this book: 'The definitive defence of democracy and, arguably, the finest piece of political writing ever published in English. Paine skewers his opponents with agile and often hilarious arguments, while laying out a fiercely convincing democratic philosophy.'

Left: Harvey Lane in Carey's time

Below: Carey's own account of his Leicester ordination as recorded in The Baptist Annual Register for 1790, 1791, 1792 and part of 1793

HARVEY LANE CHAPEL, LEICESTER.

trials of his situation.' Carey was twenty-seven and facing a major problem in church life. What should he do about the sin, the division and the bickering? Moulton would have him back easily—should he go there? But Carey, being Carey, kept at it;

> ORDINATIONS IN 1791. 519
>
> from 1 Theff. iv. part of verfe 1. *To pleafe God.* Mr. Horfley clofed in prayer.
>
> Rev. WILLIAM CAREY, Leicefter, (Extract). After I had been a probationer in this place a year and ten months, on the 24th of May 1791, I was folemnly fet apart to the office of paftor. About twenty minifters, of different denominations, were witneffes to the tranfactions of the day. After prayer, Brother Hopper, of Nottingham, addreffed the congregation upon the nature of an ordination, after which he propofed the ufual queftions to the church, and required my Confeffion of Faith; which being delivered, Brother Ryland prayed the ordination prayer, with laying on of hands. Brother Sutcliff delivered a very folemn charge from Acts vi. 4. *But we will give our-felves continually to prayer, and to the miniftry of the word.* And Brother Fuller delivered an excellent addrefs to the people from Ephef. v. 2. *Walk in love.* In the evening, Brother Pearce, of Birmingham, preached from Gal. vi. 14. *God forbid that I fhould glory, fave in the crofs of our Lord Jefus Chrift, by whom the world is crucified unto me, and I unto the world.* The day was a day of pleafure, and I hope of profit to the greateft part of the affembly.

he was a non-quitter. In fact he had a plan—a radical plan as to be expected: to dissolve the church and to start again!

In September 1790, Carey cancelled all church membership. He would reform the church by including in its new membership only those who signed a covenant promising New Testament behaviour. It was a drastic measure! Many signed up and gave themselves to a week of fasting and prayer for the 'new' church. And though the troublemakers who refused to sign spoke harshly and bitterly against Carey, yet the way was now open for the fellowship to move forward in a spirit of commitment and togetherness.

Carey had served his probationary years well, and in May 1791 he was ordained to the pastorate. Once more his close friends, Ryland, Sutcliff, and Fuller all took part. Samuel Pearce—pastor of Canon Street Baptist Church in Birmingham—preached an intense message on

Above: The cottage in Harvey Lane where Carey lived with his family from July 1789 to March 1793

'Glorying in the Cross.' From here on, despite some difficulties, numbers increased as sinners turned to the Saviour.

Carey's days were full, as he apportioned his time between the pastorate, school teaching and cobbling. He was orderly and methodical—keeping to a self-imposed timetable. On Monday he would study the classic languages, disciplining himself to translate some. On Tuesdays he would study 'science, history and composition.' Wednesdays he spent preparing studies on the book of Revelation for his midweek meeting. Thursdays he would visit friends; Fridays and Saturdays were spent in immediate preparation for the Sunday ministry. During his regular ministry at Harvey Lane, he would often speak on his passion for mission, which the church caught and turned into prayer at their regular prayer meetings.

Family life was hectic as William, Dorothy, and their four children under six—Felix, William, Peter, and Lucy—all lived in the cottage opposite the chapel. The kitchen was the hub of activity, being also the living room, workshop, and classroom! William ensured the garden looked good and his window boxes provided a splash of colour.

Tragically there was a repeat of the bitter heartbreak that struck

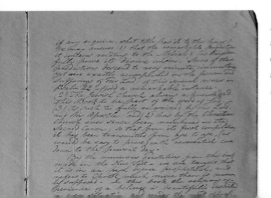

Left: Part of Carey's manuscript of his work on the Psalms. Now in the possession of the Bristol Baptist College

Left: The only remnant of Harvey Lane today— 'Harvey Walk', a footbridge over Leicester's one-way system!

in Piddington. Little Lucy died before her second birthday. Carey told his father that, 'he had been touched at a very tender point.' The grieving pastor and his wife buried Lucy in the graveyard attached to the meeting house, and we can only imagine their sadness as daily they passed near her little grave.

Hesitating in Clipston

Carey, fully stretched in church work and wider interests, still had the missionary spark within him, and still tried to ignite it in others. As in Moulton, so in Leicester he took every opportunity to cast his vision of gospel preachers going to heathen lands. He was still a part of the Northamptonshire Association of Calvinistic Baptists, so he joined them in Clipston on 27 April 1791 for some special days of worship and mutual encouragement.

Both Sutcliff and Fuller had a missionary theme bubbling in their powerful preaching. Sutcliff preached on "Jealousy for God"

from 1 Kings 19:10 and pleaded for 'hearts which embrace a globe and every habitable shore.' He daringly claimed that God's intention for the 'local congregation of believers is that it be an aggressive evangelistic body, seeking to enlighten the whole earth.' His vision was clear: 'When God's people pray and evangelise, the empire of Jesus shall advance, his kingdom arise, and the crown flourish upon his head.' Then Fuller rose to bring the next wave of truth upon men already shaken by God's word. From Haggai 1:2 he gave a 'clarion call to world mission.' For the past seven years they had been seriously praying for God to work powerfully, and yet Fuller sensed a 'procrastinating spirit' among his fellow ministers, so he addressed it and spoke of the evil of delay which resulted in few and feeble efforts being made in gospel work. He was calling for action. He mentioned the sixteenth century Reformers, and challenged his hearers: 'Since their days, we seem

Above: Clipston, a 'sleeping beauty' village

Below: Clipston Church where the Northamptonshire Association preaching meetings were held on 27 April 1791. This present building was built in 1803

to sit down half contented that the greater part of the world should still remain in ignorance and idolatry... We pray for the conversion and salvation of the world, and yet neglect the ordinary means by which those ends have been used to be

accomplished...' All present were deeply moved. Clipston's pastor, Webster Morris, commented, 'Every heart was subdued. Such deep solemnity has seldom been witnessed.'

Carey was present, his heart almost beating out of his chest as he heard these sermons. He was prepared to go further than others; he was ready to do what others only preached about. At the village inn where they were having their midday meal, Carey pressed for action 'He called for impression to be turned into expression' and homed in on his fellow ministers to do something—to start up 'a society for propagating the gospel among the heathen.'

All afternoon Carey pushed the

Above: The village inn in Clipston—today the Bull's Head—the most likely place where Carey hounded his friends to decide for mission in April 1791

logic of the morning sermons: form a missionary society. Fuller's sermon title was 'The Pernicious Influence of Delay', and infuriatingly that influence was seen that very afternoon. Though they were not against such a society, nobody was brave enough to take this further step. Sutcliff himself, now out of the pulpit, 'cautioned against haste.' Fuller, also out from behind the safety of a pulpit admitted, 'Feeling the difficulty of setting out on such an unbeaten path, their minds revolted at the idea of attempting it. It seemed too much like grasping at an object utterly beyond their reach.' Their minds knew something must be done, but they just would not do it.

However, Carey would not let the matter drop. He raised it again that night with those who were staying at the Manse in Clipston. With supper finished, Carey was still in full flow; talking missions kept him up at night. On they went beyond midnight. One o'clock came; Fuller's stomach rumbled and he asked for more food. They roasted some meat on the fire and continued into the early hours of the morning talking and eating. But still they dallied, still they held back, and once again nothing was done. The only bright outcome of that long day was the encouragement his fellow ministers gave him to finish writing his book.

'Attempt great things for God'

On Tuesday afternoon, 29 May 1792, ministers and messengers from the 24 churches of the Northampton Association of Particular Baptists began to gather in Nottingham. They stayed at the Angel Inn, in the town's market-place. The next morning at 6.00 they were at prayer in the Baptist Chapel in Friar Lane.

Then at 10.00am Carey was unleashed. For years he had been building up to this moment. He announced his text from Isaiah 54:2–3 (AV) 'Enlarge the place of thy tent, and let them stretch forth the curtains of thine habitations: spare not, lengthen thy cords, and strengthen thy stakes; for thou shalt break forth on the right hand and on the left; and thy seed shall inherit the Gentiles, and make the desolate cities to be inhabited.' His sermon called the church to action, to lift their vision over the walls of their own gardens and see the need of the nations and to go out and reach them. Carey could set ice on fire. Let there be decision, let something be done, let there be no more delay. He summed up his message in 'two plain, practical, pungent, quotable watchwords': 'Expect

Carey's Enquiry

On 12 May 1792 *An Enquiry into the Obligations of Christians, to use Means for the Conversion of the Heathen* was advertised in the *Leicester Herald*.

Into this book Carey poured his soul. He used the data he had gathered for his map to show the need of the nations. He also fine-tuned the arguments he had been using against his opposers and undermined their objections. He took what was best from his discussions and preaching over the past few years, put it all in writing and published it. It was inspiring and clear: 87 pages to stir English Baptists to reach the world. After reading, no-one could avoid the reality that the commission in Matthew 28:18–20 was binding on the church for all time. The book was on sale for the 1792 meetings of the Association in Nottingham.

Above: *The old Manse at Clipston—today a private house—where Carey kept his colleagues up, talking mission, to the early hours of the morning*

great things from God. Attempt great things for God.' It was a sermon that changed the course of mission history. Its effect was like a boulder catapulted into a lake that had not been disturbed for years. Arguably the modern missionary movement can be traced back to this source. The people listening deeply felt this sermon; Ryland commented, 'Had all the people lifted up their voice and wept... I should not have wondered, so clearly did he prove the criminality of our supineness in the cause of God.'

Before they left the next day, the ministers and messengers met together for the usual private business session. Surely here they would discuss ways of putting Carey's sermon into action? But retreating from the advance Carey had urged the day before, they built a wall around themselves yet again; they dealt with necessary, but mundane issues, and then Ryland Junior prepared to close the meeting. Once again they were going to totally ignore the call to world mission. They had all heard powerful, dynamic preaching urging them to action—and once again they were going to ignore it; no discussion, no decision, no formulation of any plan to reach the nations!

According to one person: 'Carey was in an agony of distress.' He could not understand how, after all that had been done: the booklet, the talking, the

WILLIAM CAREY, D.D.
PREACHED HIS GREAT
MISSIONARY SERMON IN THIS
BUILDING-THEN A BAPTIST
CHAPEL-ON MAY 30TH 1792.

sermon, the truth, that *still* his fellow ministers did not have the faith to do anything about the cause of God in the world. Inwardly exploding, Carey turned to his friend Andrew Fuller, and gripped his arm, saying, 'Is there nothing again going to be done, sir?' As Carey gripped Fuller's arm, so God gripped his heart. Fuller felt the need for something to be done, and he insisted that before they left they resolve to prepare a plan to form a 'Baptist Society for propagating the Gospel among the Heathens'. They agreed to discuss this at their next minister's meeting in Kettering. Carey was in raptures. Heaven was on the march.

Kettering to Kolkata

The summer of 1792 was a long one for the thirty-one year old Carey. The 2nd October could not come soon enough—the day they had set to discuss the Nottingham proposal. Weather-wise, it was a horrible day as an east wind blew, and the Northamptonshire sky hung with grey clouds that declared winter was coming; but the outlook for God's kingdom that day was glorious, a new dawn was about to break. That night fourteen men squeezed into the small twelve feet by ten back parlour in Widow Wallis' house in Kettering to discuss the proposal.

Things did not start too encouragingly. The four months

Left: Friar Lane Baptist Chapel, Nottingham, where Carey preached a sermon that has touched millions of people all over the world

Top: The Carey tablet that was fixed on the front of Friar Lane Chapel in February 1903

Left: Widow Wallis' house, Kettering, which came to be called 'The Gospel Inn' because it was used to help so many gospel preachers on their journeys. Martha Wallis was a faithful member of Andrew Fuller's church

since Nottingham had given ample time for doubts and difficulties to grow in their minds. They doubted themselves, wondering who they were to even attempt such a thing—small pastors of small flocks in small unheard of villages in inland England. They were uneasy and nervous about going forward.

Carey, knowing the track record of his fellow pastors, was ready, and had come prepared with a thrilling account of how Moravian missionaries had been used by God recently amongst the nations. Carey was an avid reader of such journals and a big admirer of the Moravians. There were not many mighty or noble amongst *them* either, yet they had seen many conversions. Carey won the day. His brothers eventually came round and by the end of the

evening they had passed a significant resolution: '*Humbly desirous of making an effort for the propagation of the Gospel among the Heathen, according to the recommendations of Carey's Enquiry, we unanimously resolve to act in Society together for this purpose; and, as in the divided state of Christendom each denomination, by exerting itself separately, seems likeliest to accomplish the great end, we name this the Particular Baptist Society for the Propagation of the Gospel amongst the Heathen.*'

They sealed their commitment to the brand new society by creating a fund. These were poor pastors who at real financial cost to themselves wrote down on slips of paper the amount they were willing to give to support world evangelisation! The papers were

2/ it is agreed that this Society be called *The Particular-Baptist Society, for propagating the gospel amongst the heathen.*

III. As such an undertaking must needs be attended with expence, we agree immediately to open a subscription for that purpose, and to recommend it to others.

N. B. The names of the subscribers and amount of the subscriptions were as follows.

Rev. John Ryland — 2.. 2.. 0
Reynold Hogg — 2.. 2.. 0
John Sutcliff 1.. 1.. 0
Andrew Fuller 1.. 1.. 0
Abraham Greenwood 1.. 1.. 0
Edward Sharman 1.. 1.. 0
Samuel Pearce 1.. 1.. 0
Mr Joseph Timms 1.. 1.. 0
————————
10.. 10.. 0

Above: The minutes of the formation of the Baptist Missionary Society on display at Moulton

collected in Fuller's snuff box and counted. The promised total came to £13 2s 6d, which was a great deal of money for those Baptist pastors (Carey's Leicester wage was less than £40 a year). It was the firstfruits of a phenomenal amount of money that would be given, as Christians in Britain and America gave generously to support the cause over the years ahead. Thirteen of the fourteen men promised specific amounts of money. Carey, leading by example as ever, made an open ended promise to give any profit he made from his book! They formed an executive of five; Fuller (secretary), Hogg (treasurer), Ryland, Carey, and Sutcliff.

At last the society that Carey had laboured so long for was born.

THE OLD MANSE

THE BULL'S HEAD

CLIPSTON

KEY TO PLACES

1 CLIPSTON CHURCH 2 THE OLD MANSE 3 THE BULL'S HEAD

TRAVEL INFORMATION

Clipston

Exit junction 19 off the M1 towards Kettering. Drive along the A14 for approx 6.5 miles (10km) and then turn south onto the A5199, going back over the A14. After 1 mile (1.5km) turn left onto the B4036 and keep going for 4.5 miles (7km) until you enter Clipston.

In Clipston it is possible to recreate the walk of that earnest day on 27 April 1791. Start at the church now standing on the same place as they had their meetings that day; walk to the old Manse, where Carey kept his brothers up half the night talking mission, and then over the fields, keeping to the footpath and shutting the gates behind you, to the Bull Inn—the probable place where Carey kept his colleagues talking mission all dinner time.

Kettering

Fuller Baptist Church with its helpful staff and members is located at 51, Gold Street. There is a Heritage Room here which contains many interesting items relating to Andrew Fuller, and also to William Carey. The church website is www.fullerbaptist.org.uk Contact Margaret Williams (☎ 01604 719187) if you wish to gain access to The Heritage Room. Ask here for directions to the 'Mission House' (Widow Wallis' home) in which The Baptist Missionary Society was formed. It is now an old peoples' home so please respect their privacy and do not call there. Opposite the Mission House is Thomas Gotch's house.

ISAIAH
54:2

JOURNEY
to INDI

⑤ The irresistible goldmine

Carey's wife, along with his church, held their breath. Things had been moving so quickly and no-one could tell what was going to happen next. Would William really go and leave them all?

The freshly formed mission society was the first of its kind. Having taken this momentous step they decided to meet again twice within a few weeks, to discuss practical issues, not least, where in the world should the society begin its work? Carey, unable to attend these meetings, sent a note telling of a man called John Thomas with whom he had been put into contact.

Thomas, recently returned from gospel work in India, was in London trying to find a team member and funds for a mission to Bengal. Carey wondered if Thomas could be the man and India the opening they were looking for. Andrew Fuller followed up the lead and arranged for Thomas to meet the other members of the society at Kettering on Wednesday 9 January 1793. The day came but, because of an injury to his foot Thomas could not attend. The Society still met and between their times of prayer and preaching they discussed where they could get a man who would go to India with John Thomas.

John Thomas, 1757–1801

John Thomas, a doctor by profession, was an enigma and a man of extremes: at times moody and sullen, at other times lively, even ecstatic. He displayed many godly characteristics: a great love for the Lord, a real hunger for his word, zeal for his work, and a deep compassion for humanity; yet at the same time he was hopeless with money, often in debt, and running from his creditors. However, it was because of John Thomas that Carey first arrived in India. In 1786 Thomas served as surgeon aboard the Earl of Oxford, but on arrival in India threw himself into missionary work, learning Bengali and helping the needy. When Thomas came back to England in 1792 to gain support for his Indian mission Carey was informed of him. Pearce-Carey (see 'Further Reading') sums up Thomas' life: 'He had been a great Christian, a great missionary, a great unfortunate, and a great blunderer.'

Above: The plaque originally on the wall of Carey's Cottage in Leicester before it burnt down in 1921

'Yes, I will go'

At some point, quite unexpectedly, towards the end of the day, the door opened and in hobbled John Thomas! He told of India's deep spiritual need and poverty; he told of false religion and hopeless pilgrimages, and yet of openings for the gospel. He read a letter from two Brahmin inquirers which included these words: 'Have compassion on us, and send us preachers and such as will forward translation.' As Carey listened he felt compelled to go with Thomas to India. There and then he volunteered! It would be unreal to imagine that Carey had not previously thought of being a missionary, but he had not yet reached the point of saying 'Yes, I will go'. Only a few months

before, on 27 November 1792, he had written to his father: 'I have only to say to that, I am at the Lord's disposal, but I have very little expectation of going myself...' But now, two months later, all had changed. Thomas had described a goldmine of souls in India—there for the finding if only someone would descend the mine. Carey's adventurous spirit rose, and his zeal for the Lord took over: 'I will go down,' he declared; then pleading with his friends, 'remember that you must hold the ropes.' They agreed to do so, and Carey pledged himself to the task.

Earnestly, they questioned Thomas regarding budget, and practical issues about living in India. They must know how much they needed and how soon the 'adventure' could begin. John Thomas was hopeless with money and not the man to ask. He gave an inadequate picture, making things seem far better than they really were, and hence the society did not fully grasp the financial cost. With the little support they had, they decided that Carey and Thomas would sail to India in early April—just three months away! Afterwards Fuller told Ryland his feelings, '...events of great consequence are in train; my heart fears, while it is enlarged, with the weight that lies upon us. It is a great undertaking; yet surely it is right.'

Facing page: The streets of Carey's Leicester, compared with today's Leicester

LEICESTER

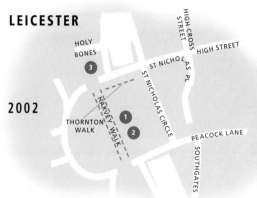

2002

1 CAREY CHAPEL (SITE)

2 BURIAL GROUND (SITE)

3 ST NICHOLAS CHURCH

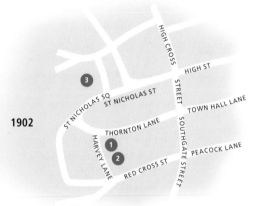

1902

1 CAREY CHAPEL

2 BURIAL GROUND

3 ST NICHOLAS CHURCH

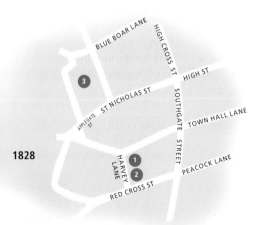

1828

1 CAREY CHAPEL

2 BURIAL GROUND

3 ST NICHOLAS CHURCH

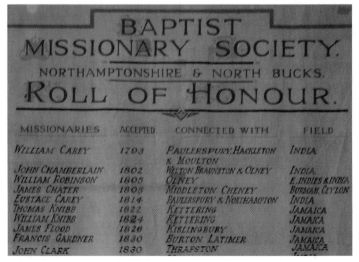

Above: The Baptist roll of Honour in the Heritage Room, Kettering. William Carey was the pioneer in a long line of brave and zealous missionaries

Facing page: Carey's communion cup now on display in Fuller Baptist Church, Kettering

All Carey had to do now was to tell his church—and his wife and children!

Breaking the news

As he made his way home William's mind rehearsed several scenarios over how to tell Dorothy of his decision to go to India. When he told her we do not know, but we do know her reaction when he eventually did—she would not go with him. It was a predictable response. Carey and his brother ministers had helped each other reach this critical point of decision over a matter of years; they had prayed about it together, preached on it and debated it. But Dorothy had some typically feminine down-to-earth questions for her adventurous visionary husband. What of the climate and the diseases? the culture and the language? the food and the money? They had three boys under eight years of age—what of the children and the voyage? Dorothy was expecting another child in early May and the thought of spending her last month of pregnancy at sea did not excite her at all! She took a sane and rational decision to say 'No; I am not going.' Far from being an adventure—Dorothy thought the whole thing crazy. Carey's father likewise thought his son's decision was 'the folly of one mad.'

Carey told his church in

Harvey Lane the following Sunday and he received the same kind of negative reaction; they were 'woe-struck', and 'sorrow manifested and reigned through the place of worship.'

Tensions

Carey was now living under unbearable tensions at home and in church. He had no support from either and in desperation called Andrew Fuller to come and speak to them both. Fuller brought Sutcliff to help him! Dorothy was still adamant. But they did have some success with the church. The meeting was negative until one brave member stood up, and reminded the church of how Carey had preached and taught on the need to go to the lost and of their prayer meetings where they had pleaded for the extension of Christ's kingdom. How could they now rebel against the word and refuse to let their pastor do the very thing they had been praying for? 'God is bidding us make the sacrifice which shall prove our prayers' sincereness'. With these words the attitude of the meeting changed, no longer did they think of themselves but of the kingdom. Carey had the thrill of seeing the fruit of the past four years of his teaching develop before his eyes. He had brought them to unity and missionary vision. And now they agreed, not just to let him go, but to send him! The church sent a letter to the Association Day in 1793 warmly commending 'Our dear and beloved pastor...to go and preach the gospel to the heathen.'

'Every time we say goodbye I seem to die a little'

The thought of leaving his wife, family and church didn't get any easier as the time drew nearer. He wrote to his sister Mary: 'I have never wavered about the duty itself, but I feel much leaving my family and people.' Dorothy and William had come to an uneasy agreement that he would take eight year old Felix, with him, live in India for four years, set up home, then return to fetch his wife and family. Meanwhile Dorothy and the children would live in Hackleton, with her younger sister Catherine.

Carey's farewell to Harvey Lane came in two parts. Sunday 17 March 1793 was his last Sunday, with packed services, eight baptisms and unbearable goodbyes to a people he had come to love dearly. Wednesday 20 March would be the final farewell

Left: Olney Baptist Church today. Carey always had a soft spot for Olney Baptist and it was one of Carey's major supporters during his time in India

Below: John Sutcliff, pastor of Olney Baptist Church during Carey's time

services for him. The men who had formed the mission met for prayer in the morning, commending Carey to the Lord. At the afternoon service John Thomas related his heart-gripping stories from India. In the evening Reynold Hogg preached from Acts 21:12–14. Finally Andrew Fuller gave an emotional charge to Thomas and Carey from John 20:21 concluding: 'Go then my dear brethren, stimulated by these prospects. We shall meet again. Each, I trust, will be addressed by our Great Redeemer, "come ye blessed of my father—enter ye into the joy of your Lord."'

The next six days were spent settling Dorothy and the children into Hackleton. Then came the dreaded Tuesday 26 March, when William kissed his wife and children goodbye for what, for all they knew, could well be the last time ever. That night William and Felix went to Olney, and held a final service at the Baptist chapel that had commissioned him to preach in the first place. William, with so much life running through his veins, preached from Romans 12:1, 'living sacrifices'. He felt his subject as he thought of his wife and family back home, and when he read out the closing hymn, by the Baptist pastor and hymn-writer Benjamin Beddome, he did so with all the emotion of a man standing on the edge of the biggest thing in the world:

'And must I part with all I have,
Jesus, my Lord, for thee?
This is my joy, since thou hast done
Much more than this for me.
Yes let it go; one look from thee
Will more than make amends

Above: *The Guildhall in Leicester dating back to the 14th century. In 1632 the Town Library was moved into the East wing. The library was still there during Carey's time, and being only about five minute's walk from where Carey lived we can imagine him often there*

> For all the losses I sustain,
> Of credit, riches, friends'.

A false start

As soon as the missionary group arrived in London they set about getting permits to enter India. Anyone caught sailing to India without a licence from The British East India Company would be forcibly returned to England. The trouble was, the East India Company discriminated against missionaries and refused permission to travel. No matter how many petitions Carey made to India House they just could not get a visa. The only way was to travel secretly and enter India as illegal immigrants! Carey and Thomas were prepared to do this, and Captain White, with whom Thomas had sailed twice before as ship's surgeon, was willing to run the risk.

On Thursday 4 April 1793, Carey with his son Felix, John Thomas and his wife and daughter; and also two of Thomas' cousins boarded the *Earl of Oxford* and set sail for India. The anticipation they felt was intense—after all the years of teaching, convincing, praying, and plodding they were off. However, France and Britain were at war with one another again, and it was dangerous to sail alone, so they anchored in the Solent and waited

Above: The old East India House, Leadenhall Street, before being rebuilt in 1726. The Lloyd's Building now stands on the same site

Below: The flag of the British East India company, formed by royal charter 31 December 1600 for conducting trade with East and Southeast Asia and India

for six long weeks for their naval escort to arrive. They spent the time in Ryde on the Isle of Wight which Carey found to be so beautiful. The nature loving Carey returned to his boyhood as he wandered the woods and viewed the sea, surveying the beauty of God's creation. The past few months and years had been so busy, but now he had chance just to be still.

After a few weeks, William received a letter from Dorothy telling him their baby had been born. He was overjoyed, and saw this as the reason for his delay in sailing to India—if he had sailed on time he might not have heard this news for months! The letter opened the wounds he had on

leaving his family, and on 6 May he wrote back telling her how much he missed her and his children: 'If I had all the world, I would freely give it all to have you and my dear children with me... Be assured I love you most affectionately.'

Two weeks later, on 21 May, Carey was writing another letter, only this time not to Dorothy, nor so positive. It was addressed to Andrew Fuller informing him of a crazy chain of events which resulted in them being thrown off the ship and prohibited from sailing to India. John Thomas, hopeless with finances, owed a lot of money to a lot of people and one of them heard he was leaving the country, informed the East India Company, who promptly

Above: Standing today on the site of the old East India House, The Lloyd's Building designed by Sir Richard Rogers and completed in 1986

told Captain White of the authorities' awareness of an illegal passenger on board and that he could lose his command if he continued to India. Whilst Thomas' wife and daughter could travel, Thomas could not, and Carey decided to stay behind with him. When the convoy eventually arrived, Carey and Thomas could only watch from shore as the *Earl of Oxford* sailed for India taking their dreams with it. And yet Carey, as a man of faith, knew this was not the end of his vision; he was confident that these strange events were 'superintended by an infinitely wise God.' And in his tears Carey bowed in humble submission.

They were cast down but not destroyed, and immediately the three of them caught a boat to Portsmouth, where they stored

Above: Carey took frequent walks in the woodlands of the Isle of Wight during his stay. Being so much in the open air again gave him good health and a large appetite, indeed he said that he could 'eat a monstrous meat supper, and drink a couple of glasses of wine after it!'

Above: The plaque on the outside wall of 40 Castle Street, Ryde

their baggage, sure that they would be sailing for India soon, and then a bumpy stagecoach ride to London to work out another way of getting to their destination.

In London John Thomas set out to redeem himself for the trouble he had caused Carey and their supporters. He tried desperately hard to get a passage to India. The fact that his wife and daughter had gone on before gave him maximum motivation. His search took him to a coffee-house on the east side of London and, knowing that no British ship would take them, he asked 'whether any Swedish or Danish ship expected to sail from Europe to Bengal, or any part of the East Indies, that season.' A waiter eventually brought him the reply: 'A Danish East Indiaman, No. 10 Cannon Street.' They lost no time and hurried to the offices, where they eventually found that a Danish boat was sailing from Copenhagen to Calcutta (now called Kolkata) and was expected to halt off Dover within five days.

Dorothy relents

The door was open to sail, and yet Carey wanted more. Dorothy was but a stagecoach ride away, he could go and see her, his children and his new baby; maybe even convince her to come with him? Despite the dangers of travelling at nightime they caught the late Friday night coach to Northampton and arrived in

Above: Marked by a plaque over the front door, 40 Castle Street, Ryde, where Carey stayed while waiting on the Isle of Wight for a Naval escort to India

Hackleton by breakfast the next morning. Carey was overjoyed to see his wife and children again, and to meet his three week old baby Jabez. But still Dorothy refused to travel to India with such a young family, and so they experienced another painful parting as once again they had to tear themselves away from each other and say their sad farewells.

Thomas could not cope with William and Felix as they made their way back to Northampton. He said he would go back and plead with Dorothy. William suggested this would only add to her heartache. But Thomas, headstrong as ever, went back and applied emotional pressure to convince her to come to India. He claimed: 'I feel impelled in love to be severe.' But it was press-ganging a woman who was in an emotionally fragile condition. He told her that if she refused to go then she would be the cause of a divided family, and that she would repent of this as long as she lived! Finally, the terrified Dorothy agreed to go—if her sister Catherine would come with her. All eyes turned to Catherine, seven years younger than Dorothy, who said she must go to her room and pray; and when she returned she said she was willing. Thomas rushed to tell William who rushed to Dorothy and the children. But it was an emotional decision forced on her by Thomas, and it would cost her and William and their family dearly for the rest of their days.

Eight people now made up the travelling party: William, Dorothy, the four boys, Catherine and John Thomas. There could be no delay

Above: Sea views near Ryde in the Isle of Wight. No doubt Carey looked longingly out over the sea waiting patiently to embark for India

as the ship was due at Dover anytime. They had only £150, refunded by Captain White, but needed around £700 for their fares and baggage. Through a hasty meeting with Ryland the money was amazingly raised. Back in Hackleton they packed at speed, sold or left what they could not take and filled two chaises and raced to London. The boys were in a whirl of excitement, Dorothy was a well of emotional grief as she said farewell to life as she knew it. John Thomas purchased the tickets in London, then caught a boat to Portsmouth to fetch their belongings. Within days they all met up at Dover.

And there they waited. The ship they were to travel on *The Kron Princessa Maria*, a Danish East Indiaman, weighing 600 tons and being 130 feet long, with sails occupying three masts and a copper bottom to enhance its speed, was delayed for two weeks. They had time to catch their breath and to assess the major decisions that had been made. The past few days had been a tornado. But now they calmly waited. Then at 3pm on 13 June the ship appeared with her frigate escort, the guns sounded to signal her arrival, and by 5pm they were all aboard for India. The white cliffs of Dover were soon behind them as they began the long voyage.

That night William wrote in his diary for Thursday, 13 June: 'This has been a day of gladness to my soul. I was returned, that I might take all my family with me, and enjoy all the blessings which I had surrendered to God. This "Ebenezer" I raise. I hope to be strengthened by its every remembrance.'

Above: *Sprawling Leicester today—totally unrecogniseable from the city that Carey knew and left behind*

Like all cities Leicester has gone through considerable development and new road systems over the years. Harvey Lane church is no longer standing and Carey's Harvey Lane cottage was destroyed by fire in 1921. Today the whole area has been reconstructed to make way for the Southgates Underpass.

Central Baptist Church, Charles Street, LE1 1LA, houses a small Carey museum in which you can see a tableaux of scenes from his life, some of his cobbler's tools, a model of his cottage, some Indian objects, and some original documents from church meetings sending him to India. The museum is open to view every Sunday or other times by prior arrangement with Mr Keith Harrison— ☎ 0116 287 3864. The web address is www.central-baptist.org.uk

Above: *Scenes from Carey's life: a tableaux at Central Baptist Church, Leicester*

⑥ Mudnabatti madness

Carey wanted to attempt great things for God, but his first seven years in India taught him that nothing great is ever easy. He faced severe trials: moving from place to place, contending with illness, madness, even death in his family. Any lesser man would have given up and gone home

William Carey and his family arrived in India on 11 November 1793, five months after leaving England. The 15,000 mile journey had the usual terrifying storms and infuriating becalms; but for Carey it also had great frustration—it was a non-stop voyage! He was 'in Europe, Africa, South America, and Asia' and longed to meet the people of these lands and experience their cultures. There were unconverted pagans in these nations; men and women who mattered to God and who needed the gospel, but they had to pass them by on their way to India.

With a big vision for the whole world, Carey pleaded with the society back home not to neglect these spiritually needy nations: 'I hope you will go on and increase, and that multitudes may hear the glorious words of Truth.

Africa is but a little way from England; Madagascar but a little further; South America and all the many and large islands in the Indian and Chinese seas will, I hope, not be forgotten.'

The *Kron Princessa Maria* entered the Hugli River and Carey rejoiced as he caught his first sight of the people he was to devote his life to. Two boats, with some very poor Indians, came out

Facing page: Sunrise above the Bay of Bengal—Carey entered India bringing the light of the gospel

Above: *A Carey and Thomas commemorative medal issued for the Jubilee of the founding of the Baptist Missionary Society at Kettering*

to sell fish. Carey commented: 'I like their appearance very much'. Thomas enquired if they had any Shastras (Hindu sacred writings)—to which they replied they were too poor to possess or read them—they were only for the educated and rich. There and then Carey's task was confirmed: to 'bring God's Shastras within reach of India's humblest, and so to promote their education, that they would be able to read them.' His vision was clear: make the word of God known so that people could be saved and society transformed.

The British in India

On 31 December 1600 Queen Elizabeth I formed the British East India Company and gave it a monopoly of all English trade to Asia. In the years that followed the company grew into an unchallengeable giant of commerce, politics and military might and became an agent of imperial expansion in the east. By 1784, a Board of Control was established to oversee the revenue, administration and diplomatic functions of the company as well as its military expansion.

Trading posts developed into major commercial towns. One such was Calcutta, where in 1756, the Muslim ruler of Bengal, Siraj Ud Daulah, provoked by the territorial expansion and the aggressive ambitions of the British, launched an attack and took Calcutta. Robert Clive (Lord Clive of India) led the British army in response and defeated Siraj Ud Daulah at the battle of Plassey in June 1757. Clive laid the foundations of the British Empire in India and certainly from this date the East India Company developed from an association of traders to foreign rulers exercising political sovereignty over a largely unknown land and people. The British East India Company was now firmly in control of much of India, and the governors of the Company's commercial settlements became governors of provinces. Warren Hastings (1773–1786) was the first Governor-General in India, followed by fourteen others—all seeking to expand British territories and rule in India. The Indian rebellion broke out in 1857, and the following year the rule of the British East India Company in India was transferred to the crown and the period of the British Raj began. This lasted until the independence of India in 1947.

Above: Clive of India. He conquered Bengal, drove the French from India and built a civil service. But was he good or bad for India?

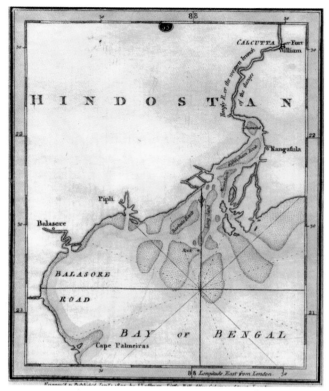

Above: The Mouth of the Ganges and the Bay of Bengal from a map of 1802

His strategy was simple: learn the language, translate the Bible into that language, educate the people to read, let the Bible loose, and watch God work. Soon people would come to Christ for salvation, worshipping the true God, and, in time, the light of the scriptures would shape society around them.

Carey was like a coiled spring ready to pounce into India, but as an illegal immigrant he and his family had to sneak in, avoiding the watchful eye of 'immigration'. They very soon came into an Indian market in full swing and had never seen anything like it—the sights, sounds, smells and colours assaulted their senses! The crowd offered them curry and rice on plantain leaves, and invited them to their villages; it was their first taste of glorious Indian cuisine. Thomas used his Bengali to preach to the fascinated crowd. The reception was full of eastern promise and Carey had high expectations of the kingdom of Christ being set up almost immediately!

Top: An Indian market today

Middle: Indian food and spices that Dorothy would have had to learn how to use

Above: The Roman Catholic Church of Our Lady of Bandel, the oldest church in Bengal consecrated by Portuguese Augustinian friars in 1599. It was destroyed by the Mughals, and rebuilt by the Portuguese in 1640

In a wilderness with no sympathy

Despite this encouragement, the first few months in India proved disastrous. Unable to stay in Calcutta (Kolkata) they moved thirty miles north to the Portuguese settlement of Bandel. Here they began gospel work in the villages and markets, but they soon hit a snag: John Thomas' creditors had caught up with him again and he needed to move back to Calcutta to use his medical skills and earn serious money to repay big debts.

Carey and his family moved down to Maniktala, where they stayed just a month but went through severe trials—Carey described it as a 'wilderness', though today it is a busy part of Calcutta. Their accommodation was appalling as they lived in a run-down, dilapidated 'garden house'. Money was scarce—they did not even have enough for the basic necessities of life; Dorothy and Felix became acutely ill with dysentery and Dorothy and her sister hated it here. When they found out that John Thomas, the man who had just about terrorised them into coming to India in the first place, was living comfortably in a big house in Calcutta with twelve servants, they felt seriously hard-done-by. Dorothy had endured the ordeal of a five month crossing caring for four boys under nine years of age; she could hardly understand a word of what was being said by the locals, the

Above: Scenes around Bandel. Carey and Thomas often went out to evangelise the villages

food was strange to her, and her husband never seemed to be at home. The pressure began to get to her, and along with her sister, she began to make William's life a misery with incessant complaining—even giving him 'abusive treatment'. William was doing his utmost to try and find money and food for his family whilst at the same time seeking to advance the gospel, but he felt all alone, not 'receiving much sympathy' from those nearest him. The whole situation was a complete mess. He was true to his missionary principles, so he would not just go and live the *European way* in Calcutta, but would live and work amongst 'the people'. Carey became dejected and lonely, having no support from anyone, not even Thomas, but his faith did not fail, and his purpose in being in India, though challenged, did not cease—he still longed to see 'in this Land of Darkness, a people formed for God'; but it was time to look to move elsewhere.

Darkness in Debhata

Carey had been offered a piece of land near Debhata, today just over the border in Bangladesh, forty miles east of Calcutta, and though Felix was still very ill, and Dorothy had reached the stage where nothing would please her but being back in England, and a third move in three months appealed to no-one, yet it seemed the best thing to do. They would live in a bungalow belonging to the Salt Department until William could build a small bamboo house for his family. They made the arrangements to move, packed up their belongings, and on 3 February 1794 set out on the dangerous three day boat journey across salt lakes and rivers to Debhata

On arrival they found yet more trouble—the promised bungalow was occupied! The words exchanged between William and Dorothy are best left unknown. The Company's Salt Assistant, Mr Charles Short, a noble unbeliever, felt sorry for them and offered accommodation in his home for as long as they needed. His brick

Above: Bengal Tiger

built bungalow, with its semi-circular veranda over-looking the lovely River Jubuna, was luxury compared with what they had known for the past few months. Felix recovered, and Dorothy became a little more accepting of the situation, though the thought of cobras snaking nearby, of fierce tigers and leopards prowling in the jungle, and of the rivers swarming with crocodiles did nothing to calm her already frazzled mind and she became paranoid over the safety of her four young boys.

Carey spent the majority of his time just across the river, a mile north, in the 'pleasant situation' of Kalutala, where he had been given a few acres of land with 'fine soil'. In his *Enquiry*, Carey laid down the principle that missionaries should 'cultivate a little spot of ground just for their support', and this was what he, and his sons, were now busy doing. They spent many happy days clearing the land in preparation for building a small house and establishing a 'little farm' which would enable them to be self-supporting. Carey loved this kind of open air work and came across all kinds of plants and wildlife never seen in Whittlebury Forest. He could have lived for this, yet his journal entries reveal that he never forgot the reason why he came to India, for example, 21 March 1794: 'The Conversion of the Heathen is the Object which above all others I wish to pursue.'

Carey had come to India to bring the light of the gospel to a people living in darkness—and in Debhata he *felt* 'heathen darkness' all around him. A temple was here where Radha and Krishna were worshipped, and at certain times of the year special festivals were held when thousands flocked to Debhata. At these times Carey observed firsthand the emptiness and even the physical harm that false religion did to his fellow human beings. He repeatedly called their actions and music 'horrid', and was aghast at their behaviour during the festivities. He longed to preach the gospel directly to them and so he intensified his Bengali language learning, and with the help of a

Above: Radha and Krishna who were worshipped in the temple at Debhata

pundit (a Hindu scholar and specialist in the classical traditions of Indian philosophy and literature) continued to translate the Bible. He made good progress in these studies, as well as on his land. Carey was settling in for the long term, when a new opportunity came.

'The valley of the shadow of death'

John Thomas was by now the manager of an indigo production plant in Moypaldiggy, and he had obtained for Carey an opening to manage a similar plant in Mudnabatti, a village thirty-two miles north of Malda up the Tangan River. Carey received a letter on 1 March 1794 inviting him to the post. It would mean a settled job with a good salary that would enable him to provide for his family and support himself in gospel work. He would be near Thomas again and he would have 'official' status in India. So having spent just under four months in Debhata, on 23 May, Carey packed up his family yet again and took them on an exciting but difficult three week, 250 mile journey through India's rivers to reach Malda on 15 June 1794. This time the travelling party would be less than before as Dorothy's sister Catharine remained behind to marry Charles Short, the man who accommodated them in Debhata.

But if things were bad at Debhata, and miserable in Maniktala, they would be utterly dire in Mudnabatti—Carey described this place as the valley of the shadow of death.

At first life started well for them as they moved into their newly built two-storey spacious house, with a large garden that Carey could delightfully develop. He was soon writing home asking for all sorts of plants, seeds, bulbs, and even trees—a request he would frequently repeat during his years in India. After a while the indigo plant was up and running, and the seasonal nature of the work meant he had many free months to devote to gospel work. He began at home in the half Hindu, half Muslim village of Mudnabatti. Every Sunday around 500 people gathered to hear Carey preach and teach the Scriptures! He had come a long way in his language learning and could preach in Bengali for up to thirty minutes by now. He widened his work circle by going out to the 200 villages of the district and could write home saying, 'over twenty miles square I have published Christ's name.' Added to this direct evangelism, he also formed two schools in keeping with his missionary strategy—to educate the locals so that one day they could read the Scriptures for themselves. By the time he left Mudnabatti his schools contained around thirty pupils from all

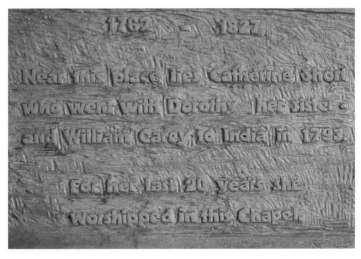

Above: The plaque in the church in Clipston, England, stating that Dorothy's sister Catharine returned there, worshipped in this chapel for the last twenty years of her life and was buried here

Above: An indigo factory. Carey's work involved ensuring the growing and harvesting of indigo plants on surrounding farms, then bringing the crop to the factory where the plants would ferment in large vats, before being dried and treated to extract a blue dye. The factory that Carey supervised required between 400 and 500 men **Inset:** Dye made from the Indigo plant. Indigo, India's major dyestuff until the mid 20th century, was widely used both locally and for export

castes, aged between five and twenty years.

The people were polite and accepting of Carey's ministry; they would regularly turn up and loved to listen, but none made any saving response to the gospel. Discouragingly, during Carey's first seven years in India he did not see one single conversion among the Indians. His heart ached, and it began to affect him spiritually and emotionally—Baptists without baptisms become sad people. He knew his supporters back home wanted to hear of conversions. Alas he could not report any, but only the hardness of the task, and how hundreds of years of tradition and superstition ruled the Indians.

Family tragedy

Within a few weeks of arriving at Mudnabatti a severe fever spread through the indigo workforce and struck Carey's family badly. Five year old Peter caught the fever and William and Dorothy had the trauma of watching him fight for his little life for two weeks before he eventually died on 11 October 1794. Peter's parents and brothers were totally devastated.

Above: The ancient and modern in today's India. The ox and its cart would have been a familiar sight to Carey

Over the past sixteen months Dorothy had suffered many hardships, hurts, losses and fears: the sad and frantic farewells in England, the long voyage with a young baby, the culture shock of India, the uncertainty of the numerous moves, the humiliation and pain of dysentery, her sister left in Debhata, and now the death of her five year old son. It all became too much for her, and she seemed to retreat from reality. When she contracted serious dysentery again sometime between January and March 1795 Dorothy plummeted deep into a mental illness that stayed with her up to her death twelve years later in 1807.

Dorothy had 'slipped across the subjective border between sanity and insanity.' She could be quite rational with some people and at some times, but then she would break into violent and abusive outbursts as she raged against William. During these

A reality check for those back home

In order for his home supporters to understand how hard his task was, Carey wrote the following words: 'Only imagine England to be in the situation of Bengal; without public roads, inns, or other convenience for travel; without post, save for the letters of the nobility; without the boon of printing; and absorbed in the monkish superstition of the eleventh century—that in this situation two or three men arrive from Greenland to evangelise the English, and settle at Newcastle—that they are under the necessity to labour for their living, and to spend much time in translating the Scriptures, and you will be able to form some idea of our case.'

Left: Street market life, little changed from Carey's day

occasions her language could become obscene, and she became highly suspicious of her husband, stalking him from place to place and openly accusing him of unfaithfulness. She even threatened to cut his throat with a kitchen knife. William wrote home to his sisters: 'My poor wife must be considered as insane, and is the occasion of great sorrow.' William and John Thomas wondered what to do; they tried various strategies to help her, but eventually, and reluctantly, they had to confine her to her room during these bouts of irrationality. A clinical psychologist, James Beck, has written: 'Today we would diagnose Dorothy's condition as a Delusional Disorder or Paranoid Disorder-Jealous Type.' During her illness William did not always react as he should, and on 7 February 1795, he wrote in his journal that he wished this day could be consigned to oblivion! What in the world happened that day? Carey's journal at this time reveals that he himself was 'overwhelmed with depression', struggling deeply in his walk with God, finding prayer hard, and feeling all alone.

The easiest thing would be to give up and go home. His marriage was a mess, (though in January 1796 Dorothy gave birth to a seventh child, Jonathan) his poor wife was ruined, he was still weak after the fever, and there was no break in the hard hearts of those around him. Yet such was Carey, that in no way would he give up the work of spreading the gospel. He had a great purpose and vision, and it was this that kept him up late at night and got him out of bed early in the mornings. He knew that 'Hindustan must be among the "all nations" which shall call Him blessed.'

But he did need help, and quickly. He wrote home saying, 'Ten thousand ministers would find scope for their powers' in India.

The Missionaries now waiting at …

The home society responded and sent reinforcements: John Fountain arrived unexpectedly on 10 October 1796; and a few years later Carey got word that a missionary party of eight adults and five children, had docked. These included William Ward, Joshua and Hannah Marshman, Mr and Mrs Daniel Brunsdon, Mr and Mrs William Grant, and John Fountain's fiancée, Miss Tidd.

But the all-powerful British East India Company would not allow them to enter India! They were impounded awaiting return to England: 15,000 miles and ordered to go straight back! They managed to get word of their predicament through to Carey, and of the only option open to them: Colonel Bie, the Governor of the Danish settlement in Serampore, had offered them protection and the opportunity to 'buy houses, establish schools, print the Scriptures, and even get passports into British territory. Above all they could preach freely.' Should they go there, and would Carey join them?

Carey had to make a quick decision. The impounded missionaries were living in terrible conditions on board ship, and

Above: *The congested streets of North Calcutta*

Facing page, above: *William Ward, the printer from Derby*

Facing page, below: *Joshua Marshman who with his wife Hannah did a great work in the schools*

horribly one of them, Mr Grant, had already died leaving his wife and two children. The decision was far from easy. Carey had been in Mudnabatti for five and a half years building up a work, starting schools, gaining the trust of the locals, and establishing contacts; should he now leave all this and go? Even more, Carey had poured a large amount of money and energy into a new indigo factory in Kidderpore, because the Mudnabatti one had to close down after a trail of disastrous results in the indigo harvest through illness, flood, and then drought!

Carey was thirty-eight and facing one of the major decisions of his life: 'It was all so affecting to my mind that I scarcely remember having felt more on any occasion soever.' By Monday 2 December, Carey had made up his mind. It was time to leave the indigo plants and move to Serampore; this was the open door that God had set before him. The family took a month to pack their belongings, close down the schools and say goodbye to contacts; for the boys it was goodbye to their friends, and for William and Dorothy it was a sad farewell to the grave of little Peter. On 1 January 1800 they set sail on their 300 mile journey to Serampore—it was a new year, and a new century—a new chapter in the gospel's advance in India was about to begin. And so he left Mudnabatti 'as lonesome a place as could be thought of.'

TRANSLATING
THE BIBLE

⑦ A red hot centre

The Danish settlement of Serampore was a beautifully calm place, but 'no sleepy hollow', indeed Carey and his team turned it into an ant's hill of activity for the gospel, and within just one year it yielded wonderful results

Carey and his group arrived at Serampore on 10 January 1800. It was a pleasant but busy port, situated on the west bank of the Hooghly river, twelve miles from Calcutta, and under the administration of Denmark. The Danish authorities dealt quickly with anything that threatened to spoil the clean and healthy environment, ensuring that this cosmopolitan place—it had as many as ten people groups making up its large population—was kept neat and tidy. The governor of Serampore, Colonel Ole Bie, had a sympathy for gospel work, and it became the major base of Carey's mission work for the rest of his days on earth.

Above: The layout of South Serampore as Carey knew it showing the details of the team's settlement. Provided by The Friends of Serampore. See their website www.friendsofserampore.org.uk.

Facing page: Panel five from the Moulton Mural depicting Carey in his Indian work. Manager of an indigo plant—Printing works—Banning Sati—Translating the Bible and Indian stories

Team work and community life

Four years before moving to Serampore, Carey had written down his vision of community life for missionaries: he pictured 'seven or eight families all living together, in a number of little straw houses, forming a line or square, and that we have nothing of our own; but all the general stock.' In Serampore he turned this vision into reality.

The Old Danish Church at Serampore in which Carey preached.   Baptist Missionary Pictorial Postcards. 19 Furnival street, EC

THE FIRST HOME
AND
PLACE OF WORSHIP
OF THE
SERAMPORE MISSIONARIES
CAREY, MARSHMAN
AND WARD
FROM 1800

Above: Plaque marking the first place of residence for the Serampore Trio. This house was later turned into Serampore Mission Church

Top: The Danish church in Serampore, built in the early 1800s, where Carey and his colleagues sometimes preached

The community included the missionaries and their families which, to begin with, were just ten adults and nine children. Over the years it grew to some sixty people including many unexpected guests. At the beginning they purchased a mission house by the river, large enough for them all to live together, though allowing them each to have their own apartments. With a lot of meekness, self-denial, and willingness to be second, they got on. Essential in their life together were their Saturday night meetings where they were open with each other, raising their concerns and grievances as well as their plans and ideas. They dealt with misunderstandings and hurts immediately. This ensured their harmony and gospel effectiveness.

Carey was the obvious leader, but it was Hannah Marshman, 'a jewel of a woman', who became the mother in the community, taking responsibility for the supplies and the cooking, as well as caring for Carey's sons, and for Dorothy whom she tended gently and lovingly. Indeed Dorothy's condition grew worse over the seven years she lived in Serampore. In letters home the missionaries made a wide range of comments about Dorothy from being 'stark mad' to 'mentally deranged', though the most frequent way of referring to her was 'Poor Mrs Carey'. William had to consider the best way of helping her. Returning to England

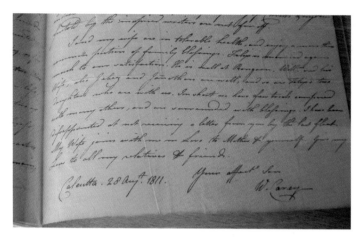

Above: Carey wrote many letters home. This is his August 1811 reply to the letter his father wrote. In possession of the Bristol Baptist College

was one option, and putting her away in the asylum that existed for Europeans in Calcutta was another; but William was convinced he was to be in India and he couldn't bear the thought of putting Dorothy in the local 'madhouse' at the mercy of 'unfeeling keepers'. The whole Serampore community shared his burden, and though they had to confine Dorothy to her room for long periods at a time, yet Hannah Marshman led the way in showing deep Christian commitment and love in caring for her during her long and distressing years of mental illness.

The missionary team formed the nerve centre of the community. They each had their own defined roles, yet they all shared the same values, strived towards the same goals, and used the same strategies. They trusted each other and were deeply committed to each other, renewing their commitment in a covenant they read out three times every year. Tragically, within eighteen months of settling at Serampore, Brunsdon and Fountain had died, but Carey found in Marshman and Ward a unity of heart and mind, of passion and zeal, that inspired him, and brought out the best in him.

The Printing Press

By March 1800 they had established a printing press which was mainly the responsibility of William Ward. This press would become a major industry, known as the Serampore Mission Press, employing fifty native craftsman to help, even manufacturing their own paper, bringing in a steam engine in 1809 to operate the mill, and, it has been suggested,

Above: The plaque on the house in Serampore where Carey was living at the time of his death (see page 102)

beginning the process of industrialisation in India.

In August 1800 they printed the first ever book in Bengali type: the gospel of Matthew. But it was on Thursday 5 March 1801 that they held a major thanksgiving service as they placed a bound copy of the Bengali New Testament on the communion table. This significant and historic moment was the fruit of years of persistent work as Carey had started translation way back in the spring of 1794. At the celebration service Carey

The eleven statements of purpose

The eleven statements of purpose of the Serampore Team's covenant—written in 1805.

It is absolutely necessary that we set an infinite value upon immortal souls.

It is very important that we should gain all the information we can of the snares and delusions in which these heathen are held.

It is necessary, in our intercourse with the Hindoos, that as far as we are able, we abstain from those things which would increase their prejudices against the gospel.

It becomes us to watch all opportunities of doing good.

In preaching to the heathen, we must ... make the greatest subject of our preaching, Christ Crucified.

It is absolutely necessary that the natives should have an entire confidence in us, and feel quite at home in our company.

Another important part of our work is to build up, and watch over, the souls that may be gathered.

Another part of our work is the forming of our native brethren to usefulness, fostering every kind of genius, and cherishing every gift and grace in them.

It becomes also to labour with all our might in forwarding translations of the sacred scriptures in the languages of Hindoostan.

That which, as a means, is to fit us for the discharge of these labours and unutterable important labours, is the being instant in prayer, and the cultivation of personal religion.

Let us give ourselves unreservedly to this glorious cause.

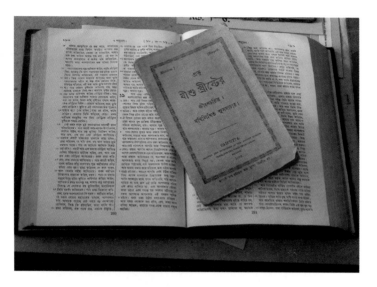

Above: A copy of Carey's Bengali Bible translation. This translation went through eight revisions until in 1832 Carey concluded 'My work is done; I have nothing more to do than wait for the will of the Lord'
Also above: The Gospel of Matthew in Bengali

preached on Colossians 3:16—'Let the word of Christ dwell in you richly', and Marshman wrote a hymn for the occasion, the second verse of which shows their intense desire and hope for this Bengali New Testament:

> 'Now shall the Hindus learn
> The glories of our King;
> Nor to blind gurus turn,
> Nor idol praises sing;
> Diffusing heavenly light around,
> This book their Shastras shall confound'.

Gospel work

The missionaries took the gospel into the open air work showing great bravery as they were vastly outnumbered, in a foreign land, and surrounded by people ardently committed to another religion. Without compromising the message they used many methods of communication including preaching, leaflet distribution, music and singing. They would go wherever 'large assemblies of natives are to be found', but they had their favourite places: the busy intersection where four roads meet, the Washermen's quarters in Rishra, and the great tree in Serampore.

Some who stopped to listen showed real interest, but neither commitment nor belief. Some argued and got more than they bargained for as Carey engaged

Carey's pulpit

them in thorough discussion, penetratingly showing up the foolishness of their beliefs and the impotence of their gods. Yet others became aggressive, throwing sticks and stones along with insults. After almost seven months of intensive gospel work in and around Serampore, William Ward wrote of the lack of response 'at present it is a dead calm; not one whisper: "what must I do to be saved."'

And then magnificently, God began to work. Carey's two eldest boys, Felix and William had become very unruly, stubborn teenagers. It was hardly surprising since Carey was too busy to look after them and Dorothy too sick. Even when Carey was with them his 'easiness of temperament'

made him 'too mild to control them.' But William Ward took a special interest in them, getting them to work with him in the Serampore print room and spending quality time with them. There came a day through Ward's witness when both Felix and William trusted Christ, and their teenage lives were changed. Carey was overjoyed as they began to work with him in spreading the gospel. But something else was on the way, something Carey had left England for.

The first fruits of a continent

Thirty-five year old Krishna Pal belonged to a Hindu sect and knew many mantras by heart, but he was still searching for the truth. On 26 November 1800 he was

Carey's medicine box   *Carey's clock*

Left: The Carey Musuem at Serampore contains a collection of manuscripts and examples of early printing in India; it also includes manuscript copies of Hindu scriptures like the Vedas and the Upanishads. Also it contains the pulpit, chairs and tables used by Carey. The library has a unique collection of early printed books in Indian and other Asian languages printed at Serampore

washing in the River Hooghly when he fell awkwardly, dislocating his shoulder. John Thomas, along with Marshman and Carey came to help. They tied him to a tree and forced his shoulder back into place all the while speaking scriptures to him and then leaving Pal to recover and think over the verses. Later in the day Thomas and Marshman went to see Pal again and gave him some leaflets in Bengali, that told of the way of salvation. The words in the leaflet rhymed like his mantras— *Sin confessing, sin forsaking, Christ's righteousness embracing, the soul is free*—and Pal could not get them out of his mind. The next day Carey took him to the Mission for some pain relief, and from then on Pal attended daily for spiritual instruction. What he learned there he took home and told his wife and her sister. Soon a group of earnest inquirers formed around Pal, listening seriously to the Bible studies given by the Serampore team. About a month later Thomas met him on the street and asked him directly whether he understood what he had been taught. Pal responded in such a way that showed he had faith in the Lord Jesus Christ, and that not only he, but also his friend Gokul, believed. The missionaries were ecstatic. John Thomas penned these words: 'Sing, soul, sing. Sing aloud! Unutterable is my gladness … It seems to me the joy will never cease. O angels, see! Oh, this is bliss!'

Eight and a half years after

Carey stood in an English church in Nottingham urging people to expect great things from God and attempt great things for God, seven years since Carey landed in India, and after so many discouragements, obstacles and setbacks—after so much plodding and persisting and lives lost, the day came for the baptism of the first Indian convert: Sunday 28 December 1800. At 1.00 in the afternoon they gathered at the riverside opposite the mission gate. The Danish governor was there, along with a number of Europeans, and many Hindus and Muslims. They sang *Jesus and shall it ever be, a mortal man ashamed of Thee?* Carey preached in Bengali, explaining baptism and making sure he drowned any ideas of the water being special or sacred. Carey then went down into the water and first of all joyfully baptised his own son Felix! Then Krishna Pal went into the water and Carey baptised him. There were tears of joy, and awe and wonder, and in heaven too there was rejoicing.

But sadly not everybody was there: John Thomas had become mentally unstable and he could

Krishna Pal's letter to the supporting churches in England

'To the brethren of the Church of our Saviour Jesus Christ, our souls' beloved, my affectionately embracing representation. The love of God, the Gospel of Jesus Christ, was made known by brother Thomas. In that day our minds were filled with joy. Then judging, we understood that we were dwelling in darkness. Through the door of manifestation we came to know that sin confessing, sin forsaking, Christ's righteousness embracing, salvation would be obtained. By light springing up in the heart we knew that sinners, becoming repentant, through the sufferings of Christ, obtain salvation. In this rejoicing, and in Christ's love believing, I obtained mercy. Now it is in my mind to continually dwell in the love of Christ: this is the desire of my soul. Do you pour down your love upon us, that, as the chatak, we may be satisfied—the bird that opens its bill, when it rains, and catches the drops from the clouds. I will tell to the world that Christ hath saved me. I will proclaim His love with rejoicing. Christ, the world to save, gave His own soul! Such love was never heard; for enemies Christ gave His own soul! Such compassion, where shall we get? For the sake of saving sinners He forsook the happiness of heaven. I will constantly stay near Him. I will dwell in the town of joy. Krishna.'

Above: The place of Krishna Pal's baptism in the Ganges. Carey counted it a great joy to 'desecrate the Ganges by baptizing the first Hindu convert' there

Facing page below: Krishna Pal, the first Indian convert

not quite cope with the ecstasy he experienced at Pal's conversion. For his own safety he had to be contained in the school; in the future they would have to move him to an asylum in Calcutta. Also, Dorothy, who had made so many sacrifices to come to India, was unable to attend her son's baptism. But for most, it was a day of rejoicing, and as the missionary community reflected that night on this massive event they knew that Krishna Pal was just the first fruits, and 'that a continent was coming behind him.'

The gospel spreads

Krishna Pal witnessed and preached wherever and whenever he could and God used his powerful testimony. He built a 'preaching hut' for around forty people, and he urged his fellow Indians to turn to Christ. He used his own home for gospel purposes, his living faith became contagious, and he became a key person in the advance of the gospel around Serampore, and eventually in Calcutta.

Within two weeks of his baptism, Krishna's sister-in-law Jaymani was baptised, and a month later, Krishna's wife

Rasamayi and her friend, Annada. A few months later Krishna's friend Gokul was also baptised and in the years that followed many more people came to Christ and professed him through baptism. There was a whole range of opposition of course, from name calling, taunting and hissing, to violence and even, in some cases, kidnapping. But Pal and Carey plodded on in gospel work, and by 1821 over 1,400 new Christians—half of these were Indian converts—had been baptised. Carey and his team marvelled and they knew that no-one else but God could have brought this about.

Carey's pastoral heart meant that he would never be satisfied with just *converts to Christianity*—he wanted to make *disciples of Christ*, and fuse them together into a church. Here Carey insisted on equality, all should take communion together, all should fellowship together, all should worship together and all should eat together. This meant his Hindu converts breaking caste. In fact Carey refused to baptise anyone who continued to maintain caste distinctions, and would not allow the caste system into the church. This had a powerful impact in their celebrations of the Lord's Supper—the untouchables with the Brahmins—even the Brahmins serving the untouchables! This was a major stand for Carey's converts, causing them much rejection and pain in Indian society, but real joy and fellowship in the body of Christ.

Serampore College

Carey, Marshman and Ward all longed to see the triumph of the kingdom of Jesus in India. They were not content with seeing a few Indians trickle into the kingdom. What they longed for was the kingdom to burst forth like a flood on India, for thousands to be

Above: *Serampore college main building shortly after construction*

Above: Serampore college main building today

saved, and for Indian society to be changed for Christ; but they knew it would not come about suddenly. It would take years of sowing the word of God before Indian life and Indian people were transformed for Jesus. Carey also knew that India would not be won for Christ just by Europeans coming as missionaries, but by Indian converts being carefully trained and equipped, who could themselves reach their own countrymen for Christ. In 1805 he wrote, 'It is only by means of native preachers that we can hope for the universal spread of the Gospel throughout this immense continent.'

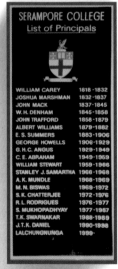

SERAMPORE COLLEGE
List of Principals

WILLIAM CAREY	1818 -1832
JOSHUA MARSHMAN	1832-1837
JOHN MACK	1837-1845
W. H. DENHAM	1845-1858
JOHN TRAFFORD	1858-1879
ALBERT WILLIAMS	1879-1882
E. S. SUMMERS	1883-1906
GEORGE HOWELLS	1906-1929
G. H. C. ANGUS	1929-1949
C. E. ABRAHAM	1949-1959
WILLIAM STEWART	1959-1966
STANLEY J. SAMARTHA	1966-1968
A. K. MUNDLE	1968-1969
M. N. BISWAS	1969-1972
S. K. CHATTERJEE	1972-1976
R. L. RODRIGUES	1976-1977
S. MUKHOPADHYAY	1977-1987
T.K. SWARNAKAR	1988-1989
J.T.K. DANIEL	1990-1998
LALCHUNGNUNGA	1999-

By the beginning of 1816 Carey and the team were talking about building a college! They all had a passion for education, and Joshua and Hannah Marshman were already doing a great work in the schools they had established in Serampore. But the vision for the college was far bigger than anything they had ever dared dream. It would be a college where Eastern literature, Western sciences and Biblical learning could be combined; a college where Indian converts could be educated in such a comprehensive way that they could go into society preaching the gospel thoroughly. It was to be

Carey,   Marshman   Ward

The Serampore Trio

Carey first met William Ward (1769–1823), a newspaper printer and then an editor from Derby, the week before he sailed to India. With typical vision and forward planning Carey challenged Ward to come to India and print the Bible once Carey had translated it! Six and a half years later, in November 1799 Ward arrived in India, and took charge of the printing at Serampore. He was 'an outspoken and at times daring proponent of social and political reform', having sympathies with the French Revolution. But he was also a personal evangelist, visiting Indian villages and leading many to the Lord, including two of Carey's own sons. He married the widow of missionary John Fountain. William Ward died in March 1823 from cholera. Carey once testified, 'Ward is the very man we need. I have much pleasure in him, and expect much from him.'

Joshua Marshman (1768–1837) and his wife Hannah (1767–1847) were a powerful man and wife team for the Lord. They both joined Carey in November 1799. Hannah Marshman proved to be a gem, a great organiser and a real mother to the team. Though struck by repeated tragedy herself (six of her children died), she continued to closely care for Dorothy Carey, as well as looking after other young missionary widows and their families. She had a burden for Indian women who did no more than 'boil their rice and bathe their children.' In 1800 she took the radical move of starting a girls' school which in fact became so successful that over the next hundred years fourteen other similar schools were built on her model. She has been called the 'First woman missionary to India and brilliant educator.'

Joshua Marshman was a scholarly man who had a heart for education and found his role in the Serampore team in running the schools. He opened two boarding schools (which helped cover the costs of the mission) and one free school for Indian children. He spent time preaching, and also raising funds for the mission. At times his manner and sharp tongue came in for a lot of criticism from the new missionaries. But Carey said of him: 'I have worked with Dr Marshman for 18 years... Marshman's excellencies are such that his defects are almost concealed by them.'

Left: The Marshman family tomb at Serampore

Below: The tablet for Hannah Marshman at the Serampore Mission Church

a college where they could learn to 'out-Sanskrit the pundits'.

In an 1817 letter to John Ryland, Carey reveals the vision behind the college: 'The work of duly preparing as large a body as possible of Christian Indians for the duties of pastors and itinerants is of immense importance. ... India will never turn from her idolatry to serve the true and living God, unless the grace of God rests abundantly on converted Indians to qualify them for mission work, and unless, by those who care for India, these be trained for and sent into the work. In my judgement it is on native evangelists that the weight of the great work must ultimately rest.'

They wanted the college to be open to Indians from any and every caste, and from any and every social standing, no matter what they had or did not have—they wanted to teach the poorest as well as the richest. The college was as 'free as the air' with no-one deprived for lack of money or background, and all lessons would be in the Indian languages so that no-one had to learn English first. The original charter declared that 'no caste, colour, or country shall bar any man from admission into Serampore College.' They admitted non-Christians who would go on to be schoolmasters, writers, journalists, lawyers so that God's truth could influence Indian society as widely as possible.

The very size of the vision was stunning—so let the college buildings match the vision. Over eight acres of land would be needed. Let the buildings be big enough for 200 students and let the college be impressive because God's truth is impressive. The college produced its first prospectus in 1818, and the main building was eventually completed by 1822. It was 'the noblest of its kind in India.' In 1827 the King of Denmark (King Frederick VI) granted a royal charter to enable the college to award degrees in all faculties—making this the first Indian college to confer divinity degrees. Today the college is still a hub of learning having over a hundred theology students studying alongside two and half thousand arts, science and commerce students, and is affiliated to Calcutta University.

Carey the botanist

Carey's boyhood love of nature came with him to India and he established a massive 'garden'—a five-acre arboretum—at Serampore in which he planted all kinds of shrubs and trees. He was continually writing home in detailed terms asking for seeds and bulbs to be sent him, giving precise details on how to pack them so they would not be ruined on the voyage. Likewise, wherever he sent missionaries he asked them to send back samples of plants and seeds from those countries. He had 427 species of plants in his garden! He imported: eucalyptus, mahogany, deodar, teak and tamarind trees. His 'garden' gave him much pleasure and proved a great stress-reliever. When it was destroyed in 1823 by devastating floods he typically set to restoring his ruined garden. In 1820 he founded the Agri-Horticultural Society in India, and contributed a twelve-page introduction to Dr. William Roxburgh's *Hortus Bengalensis, or a Catalogue of the Plants Growing in the Honourable East India Company's Botanic Garden at Calcutta,* as well as editing it and providing botanical descriptions. Roxburgh was an eminent botanist and Superintendent of the Botanic Garden in Calcutta from 1793 to 1815. The book was published at the Mission Press in Serampore in 1814. In 1823 the Linnean Society of London elected Carey as a fellow.

Pictured: Carey's house in Serampore and part of his gardens

Left: The grand Staircase in Serampore College given by the Danish Royal Family

Below: William Carey, aged fifty

Far beyond Serampore

In August 1806 Carey wrote of his desire to reach Orissa, Kurnata and Mahratta in the south of India; Hindustan, Nepal, Bhutan and Tibet in the North West; Assam, Burma, and the Malay Isles in the north-east and east; and, he added, China was only 600 miles away! Carey wanted to win as many people as possible in as many places as possible. He and his team looked on their Serampore base as a 'red-hot centre from which the light and influence of Christianity might radiate throughout a gradually widening circle.'

He was inspired by the missionaries who stopped off at Serampore to meet him and learn from him for a while, before going on to other lands. Some of these missionaries stayed for weeks, among them were men like Henry Martyn who went on to Persia, and Adoniram Judson who eventually went to Burma.

Carey developed a strategy to reach much of India by planting mission stations two hundred miles apart, throughout the country. These stations would be served by both a missionary and an Indian pastor or evangelist, and Carey would frequently plead for 'volunteers for the outfields.' By the time Carey died there were 19 mission stations established in India.

But he also wanted to go further than India. In the summer of 1807, he ordained his son, twenty-one year old Felix, and sent him out to Burma. Around 1808 he wrote that he had 'been contemplating a mission to the Afghans of Kabul.' In 1813, he ordained and sent out another son, Jabez, to Amboyna, in the Moluccas. Carey wrote to Ryland—who was by this time principal of the Baptist College in Bristol: 'Hindustan needs ten thousand ministers of the Gospel; and China as many.' He saw

England as having done much for the spread of mission, but needing to do more—he urged the home churches to have a strategy and plan to raise up and train missionaries to send abroad. Carey had a big vision and was very demanding.

Tensions back home

Sadly, his home supporters did not always share Carey's large vision. Over time the home council in England was changing. Those who were with him at the beginning on those memorable nights in Clispton and Kettering—those who became the strong and faithful rope holders who never let Carey down—were passing away (John Sutcliff died in 1814; Andrew Fuller in 1815; and John Ryland, Jr in 1825), and they were being replaced by others who did

not know Carey personally and did not quite see things his way. Even during the days of his close friends they often thought Carey a 'dreamer', but some of the new men did not even share the dream. Men who had no personal acquaintance with Carey began to run the society, and the relationship between Carey and the mission society at home became strained. They were even thinking of shrinking the work, not expanding it, and Carey wrote home outraged: 'I entreat, I implore you in England not to think of the petty shop-keeping plan of lessening the number of stations so as to bring them within the bounds of your present income, but to bend all your attention and exertion on increasing your finances so as to meet the work's pressing opportunities and demands. If our objects are large, the public will contribute to their support. If you contract them, their liberality will contract itself in proportion.'

Carey's Nottingham statement—*Expect great things from God, attempt great things for God*—still controlled him: not budgets or narrow thinking. He was not one to hold back and work within his own resources, but a man of faith who knew God's resources. And a surprising opportunity was about to come his way which, if taken, could expand the kingdom even more.

Above: The tomb of William Ward at Serampore

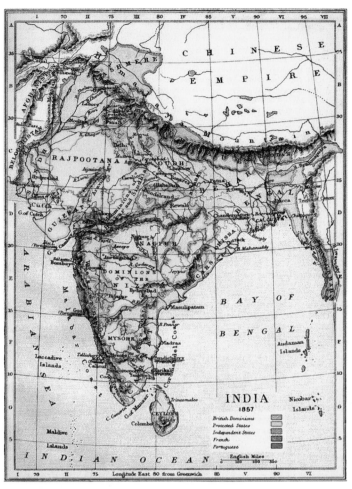

Above: A map of India dated 1857—at the height of the British Raj

Above: A marble bust of William Carey at the Metcalfe Hall of The Agricultural and Horticultural Society of India, which he founded in 1820

❽ Calcutta dreams

On Wednesday 8 April 1801, William Carey received an unexpected and official letter. It was a letter that would put him in a position to advance the gospel in India in ways that he had could never have imagined

In Carey's day the British East India Company governed Bengal. Many of their officers were raw young teenagers coming straight out of the privileged families in England and were thrown immediately into positions of responsibility throughout the districts of Bengal. Lord Wellesley, the British Governor-General, saw the need to train and educate these boys in all things Indian: its history, culture, literature and language—anything that would help them govern better. So Wellesley established Fort William College, which would run a two year training course for newly arrived civil servants. He established a department for each of the major languages and cultures of India, twelve in all. Choosing his staff carefully, he was eager to appoint William Carey to head the Department of Vernacular Languages.

Carey, opened the letter, read it, and after thought, prayer and discussion with his team, agreed this was a divine moment to seize and so he accepted, and became

Above: Panel Eight from the Moulton Mural depicting Carey's life achievements. Serampore college— first Indian baptism—working with lepers—botanic gardens

Facing page: Every hour in Calcutta today is 'rush-hour'

Above, left: Lord Wellesley, British Governor General from 1797 to 1805, who turned the Company's Bengal state into an Indian empire
Above, right: Fort William, completed in 1781, housed the main military garrison in Calcutta, and within its complex of buildings Lord Wellesley based his training college

Professor in Bengali (though because he was a non-conformist he began with the title 'tutor'). Carey kept this post for thirty years, giving a few days every week to its tasks. He excelled in his position and was soon appointed to teach Sanskrit and Marathi; also becoming the Bengali translator to the Government where, amongst other things, he translated official legal documents. And so came about one of God's superb ironies: Carey was in the Government's service, teaching the very Company—that banned him from India—how to rule India.

Carey's appointment caused raised eyebrows back home in the safe and cosy committee meetings of the English Baptists. They could not see that the post Carey had been appointed to at Fort William gave him a position of influence and respect in India and that Carey was determined to use

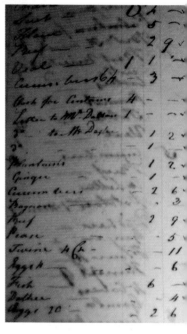

this for the advance of the gospel. Even though he might not be able to engage in direct evangelism during his classes, yet he could use his translations of the scriptures as textbooks, and in the evenings

Right: Carey sitting at his desk, surrounded by books, translating the Scriptures with his pundit. The Bible lies open at Acts 2:11 and the words in Sanskrit tell of speaking in tongues the wonderful works of God

Facing page, below: The Serampore account book kept by the Serampore Trio shows how open and meticulous they were in keeping track of their finances

he could invite his students—boys who would soon be men in significant places of authority and influence in India—to his rooms to discuss spiritual matters. An added bonus was the money this position paid—money Carey poured into the work back at Serampore.

But the men back home could not see this, and they began to interfere by giving instructions concerning personnel placements and the use of finances in India. As they tried to take control, the tone of their letters became official and authoritarian; in return Carey replied with some fairly strong letters. Years of tension eventually resulted in Carey and his team making a 'declaration of independence'

from the mission on 17 March 1827. This was a painful time for Carey, who detested disunity and felt personally hurt and let down. Perhaps this was one of the main reasons why he never returned to England.

Bible translation

Carey—ever quick and open to gospel opportunities—was not slow to see God's providence in placing him in Fort William College. Here he was surrounded by the top scholars and linguists across India. Each department had a professor, two assistant teachers and the cream of pundits in the land. Carey worked with them, and many of them worked for him. He wrote, 'I constantly avail myself of the help of the

Translations of the Bible from the Serampore Press

Carey's Bible translations were a real team effort. In Calcutta, he worked hard to understand new languages, and then with his team of Indian pundits (scholars) translated the Bible into those languages. Meanwhile in Serampore, William Ward and his team designed and cast fonts and types for that language; typesetting then took place and eventually the printing. The finished product of any translation was the result of many, many hours of teamwork.

They published their translations as soon as they had completed an individual book or portion of the Bible. Following, is a list of dates when new language translations came from the press. Additional portions of Scripture were added to these same languages over the years.

1801—Bengalee New Testament—2000 copies
1805—Mahratta Gospel of Matthew—465 copies
1809—Orissa New Testament—1000 copies
1809—Sungskrit* New Testament—600 copies
1811—Hindostani New Testament—1000 copies
1811—Persian—The Four Gospels—500 copies
1812—Printing Office and Printing materials consumed by fire!
1813—Hindee—The Pentateuch—1000 copies
1814—Sikh or Punjabee New Testament—1000 copies
1815—Burman Gospel of Matthew—2000 copies
1819—Malay Gospel of Matthew—500 copies
1821—Telinga—The Four Gospels—1000 copies
1821—Kunkun New Testament—1000 copies
1821—Pushtoo, or Afghan, New Testament—1000 copies
1822—Assamese—The Pentateuch—1000 copies
1822—Chinese Old Testament 6400 copies
1822—Bruj—The Four Gospels—3000 copies
1823—Moultanee New Testament—1000 copies
1823—Gujuratee New Testament—1000 copies
1823—Kashmere New Testament—1000 copies
1823—Bikaneer New Testament—1000 copies
1823—Nepal New Testament—1000 copies
1823—Bhugelkhund New Testament—1000 copies
1823—Marwar New Testament—1000 copies
1823—Kurnata New Testament—1000 copies
1823—Harotee New Testament—1000 copies
1823—Kanooj New Testament—1000 copies
1824—Jumboo New Testament—1000 copies
1824—Magudh New Testament—1000 copies
1824—Oojein New Testament—1000 copies
1824—Bhutneer New Testament—1000 copies
1824—Munipoor New Testament—1000 copies
1824—Khasee New Testament—500 copies
1824—Shreenagur New Testament—1000 copies
1824—Palpa New Testament—1000 copies
1824—Kemaoon—Colossians—1000 copies

*Sungskrit=Sanskrit

*Left, top:
Calcutta in
Carey's time.
Calcutta is the
capital of the
state of West
Bengal, in
northeast India.
The city was
founded by the
British around
1700 and was the
capital of British
India until 1911*

*Left, below:
Northern
Calcutta today*

most learned natives, and should think it criminal not to do so...' By the end of 1803 he had set himself a massive target: 'We have it in our power, if our means would be for it, in the space of about fifteen years to have the Word of God translated and printed in all the languages of the East... on this great work we have fixed our eyes.'

Carey was determined in Bible translation, working long hours, and taking pains to select the right words and to relay the right sense in the translation. He was meticulous in his method: he checked his work with his pundits and colleagues, and then retranslated until he was as accurate as he could possibly be. Though the work was demanding yet it was a labour of love, and far from tiring him out, this work energised him—he could do it all day and night. He wrote to Fuller: 'I am more in my element translating the Word of God than in any other employment.'

Carey soon identified Sanskrit, the sacred language of the Hindus, as the most important language, it being the base of many other Indian and Asian languages. He published his first edition of the Sanskrit New Testament in 1809, and ten years later the Old Testament. There is disagreement on the exact figures, but it seems that by the time Carey died he, along with his teams of pundits, had translated the full Bible into eight languages, the New Testament into twenty-seven, and portions of the Old Testament into ten other languages. It has been calculated that over a period of thirty years, a total of 212,000 items came off the Serampore press in forty different languages. Whatever the exact final figure it was a stellar achievement for the country lad from Paulerspury.

Targeting social abuse

Carey also used his strategic position in Fort William to pressurise for radical and far-reaching social changes in India. Though he would never be deflected from the great work of preparing people for heaven, yet at the same time he was deeply committed to doing good to people during this life. He saw the spread of the gospel as a key to social change. He was a gospel-driven social reformer. In his *Enquiry* published years earlier, he had expressed a longing for people to be made 'useful members of society'. He took any possibility to better civilization, and the Fort William professorship gave him many such windows of opportunity.

Infanticide was one of the first areas that Carey helped change. Many childless Indian women made vows to the 'Holy Ganges

Above: Infanticide as it was practiced in the Ganges

River' that if they were blessed with two children, they would sacrifice one back to the River. They did this by sliding their babies down the mud bank into the water where they would drown or be devoured by crocodiles. Carey could not stand this waste and abuse of human life—made in the image of God—and he protested to Governor-General Wellesley. A study was called for, and Carey readily presented an exhaustive report. By 1804 infanticide had been banned. He also turned his attention to abuse at the other end of human life and he cried out against the *euthanasia* practised by many families as they left the old and infirm to die on the steps leading down to the River Ganges.

Carey was outraged by the way *lepers* were treated. Many were burnt, some were drowned, and some buried alive; he helped set up a leper asylum as a positive alternative. He was also instrumental in ending *sati*. He

Above: Calcutta street market

first came across *sati* in 1799, thundered against it, called it sheer murder and determined to 'hit this thing hard.' *Sati* was the practice of burning alive a widow on the funeral pyre of her deceased husband. The belief was that she could win eternal happiness and also gain blessings for her family. The reality was that it solved a social embarrassment for families not knowing what to do with very young widows. In 1802, at the request of Lord Wellesley, Carey researched widow burning and discovered that in one year within a thirty mile radius of Calcutta there had been 438 widow burnings! For the next two and a half decades Carey spoke and wrote against *sati*. Then, when in 1828, an evangelical Christian, Lord William Cavendish-Bentinck, became Governor-General of India, he legislated against *sati*. Though there was much opposition from Indians, yet on Sunday morning 6 December 1829 the official document arrived for Carey (as the Government's Bengali translator) to translate. He spent the whole day in doing so, taking the greatest care to get it right, and by evening it was finished. Carey, the same man who first protested to the government against *sati* 27 years before, was now translating the edict to have it outlawed.

Carey contributed to the improvement of Indian life in multiple ways (see box on page 122), and this is recognised by many in India today. He translated Indian classics and was

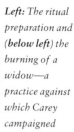

Left: The ritual preparation and (below left) the burning of a widow—a practice against which Carey campaigned

Below: Lord Cavendish Bentinck who, while Governor-General 1828–1835, legislated against sati

instrumental in the beginnings of modern Bengali literature, producing six grammars: Bengali, Sanskrit, Marathi, Punjabi, Telugu and Kanarese; and three dictionaries: Bengali, Marathi and Sanskrit. On 1 April 1818, he and his team began to publish a monthly magazine, the *Dig Darshan* (Showing the Direction), the first ever in Bengali, followed on 23 May by the first ever Bengali weekly newspaper, The *Samachar Darpan* (News Mirror). They also published the *Friend of India*, a monthly magazine aimed to give Europeans an understanding of Indian culture, problems and ways of Indian life. These papers also gave Carey and his team a voice among the people of Calcutta.

Lal Bazar

Whilst Carey knew the value of bringing the gospel to bear on public life, and the blessing that a Christian conscience can have on society, yet he never lost sight of the need for direct evangelism, and he longed to plant a church in busy Calcutta. William Ward wrote, 'Should a native church be formed there (Calcutta) and flourish so as to have active members who would

1993 Bicentenary stamp

On 9 January 1993 the Department of Posts in India issued a first day cover and stamp to mark William Carey's Bicentenary (1793–1993). Part of the brochure reads: 'The Department of Posts is privileged to issue a stamp on Dr. William Carey, who adopted India as his country and strived to serve her people. The stamp design depicts Dr. William Carey's portrait at his writing desk, against the backdrop of Serampore College.'

labour in the cause, the news of the Gospel would rapidly spread from thence into the remotest part of the country.'

Carey had this vision as early as 1802 but it was not until 26 February 1806 that a plot of land was purchased in a notoriously corrupt area called Lal Bazar. Here sin was part of the very atmosphere; it was the hotspot for drinking, prostitution and wild living—the place sailors visited when on shore. But this was a great place to plant a church to show what God can do through a community of renewed people. Three years later the first nonconformist chapel in Calcutta was opened on New Year's Day 1809.

Carey ensured that even the building made a strong statement for God. He had seen the 'religion-inspired-ugliness' of the Hindu pilgrim centres all around him, and he wanted this Christian centre to show 'God-made beauty.' He made the approach to the front doors attractive: there was a wide paved walkway from the gates to the building, and neatly arranged plants, shrubs and flowers either side of the path. When a person turned from the tempting sights and sounds of Lal Bazar into the serenity of this garden they were prepared for worship before they even reached the building.

The Sunday morning prayer meetings were packed, and during the day there were two services in Bengali and three in English. By 1810 there were more than 200 members on the church roll and there were many baptisms: sixty in 1811 alone!

The chapel became vibrant in reaching out beyond its four walls. Its members held services in the Calcutta Jail and also amongst the soldiers in Fort William, resulting in eighty seven soldiers being baptised between 1809 and 1814. It became a missionary sending church with thirty members giving themselves to missionary work in the first fifty years of the chapel! And in keeping with Carey's heart for the poor and needy, Joshua Marshman preached a sermon on Christmas Day 1809 that resulted in the Benevolent Institution for children—without any distinction of race, language or religion—opening further along in Bow Bazar Street, and doing a great work for children for nearly eighty years.

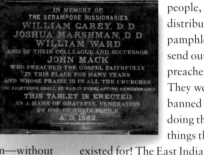

Banned from preaching

The gospel was succeeding, the kingdom of God was advancing—the Evil One would not be sleeping: wave upon furious wave of hindrances and setbacks broke over Carey and his team.

On 26 August 1806 Carey was summoned to the Supreme Court and instructed that the 'Mission preach no more to the native people, nor distribute pamphlets, nor send out native preachers.' They were banned from doing the very things they existed for! The East India Company were edgy after a mutiny in the south of India and they feared that the missionaries would incite rebellion by interfering with Indian beliefs.

Top: *Lal Bazar Chapel is now Carey Baptist Church, and still a very active church, though the building itself is a little different from Carey's time. The pillars standing at the gate are the original ones, but in 1886, the present imposing porch was added, and the steps were shortened. The wide verandah that runs the length of the church is still the same as in Carey's time, but the entrance to the church is now by swing doors at each end of the verandah instead of by a central door as in Carey's day*

Above: *Plaque marking where Carey preached in Lal Bazar*

Above: The entrance to Carey Baptist Church today, located at Ganguly Street Calcutta

Carey neither promised to obey nor disobey the order, but took it to the team for prayer.

They showed great patience and wisdom over the months that followed, and eventually Carey managed to get a twenty minute audience with the Governor-General Lord Minto, and handed him a written account detailing the fruit the gospel produces. Lord Minto read of a hundred Indians, both Moslem and Hindu, who had been baptised and how these people lived in harmony and unity together. He read of what the gospel can do to unite diverse people and to bring peace. Within a month of this audience the orders to stop spreading the gospel had been revoked. The fruit of the gospel spoke for itself!

Fire at Serampore

A few years later they faced another fiery trial. Carey was in Calcutta on 12 March 1812 when he heard urgent banging on his door. He opened it to find Joshua Marshman looking exhausted and bewildered. At 6pm the day before, there had been a raging fire in the mission printshop at Serampore; they had battled for four long hours to get it under control, but then someone opened a shutter and immediately the fire started again and a 'twenty-feet sheet of flame' burnt out of control. The furious fire spread and even threatened the dormitories of the boys and girls school and other home buildings—but thankfully no-one was killed. By 2.00 in the morning the fire had burnt itself out. Marshman then rushed to Calcutta to tell Carey of the catastrophe: the fire had almost completely destroyed the 200ft long, 50ft wide print room!

So much had been lost: Carey's manuscripts, and ten Bible translations! Including all the Kanarese New Testament; Carey's translation of the epic *Ramayana,* as well as his all-but-completed grammars and Sanskrit dictionary; over a thousand reams of English paper had burnt up, and fonts in Tamil, Chinese, Persian, Arabic, Nagari, Telugu, Bengali, Burmese, Marathi, Punjabi, Oriya, and Kashmiri, had melted in the heat. The monetary cost would be enormous—but the time cost more: days, months, weeks and years of work had been destroyed. After Carey returned from walking over the still

smouldering ruins he wrote, 'In one short evening the labours of years are consumed.'

But his faith did not fail and the team persevered. The next day they gathered the sixty-strong workforce together and told them their plan: to move to new buildings and start again! Some things had been salvaged, but a fresh start would be needed; quitting was not an option. Carey wrote home to Ryland: '... another leaf of the ways of providence, calling for the exercise of faith in Him Whose Word, firm as the pillars of Heaven, has decreed that all things work together for good to them that love God. Be strong, therefore, in the Lord. He will never forsake the work of His own hands.' And the next Sunday

Above: Inside Carey Baptist Church today

Top: Lord Minto, Governor General 1807–1813

Above: *Carey's spectacles and their case. Now in the possession of the*
Bristol Baptist College

Carey preached from Psalm 46:10: 'Be still, and know that I am God', bringing out two relevant points: 1. God's right to dispose of us as he pleases. 2. Man's duty to acquiesce in His will. By the end of July they were printing again, and by April 1813, a little more than one year after the fire, they were actually printing in more languages than before.

Death and marriage

William was always incredibly busy, yet he thrived on busyness: 'Few people know what may be done till they try, and persevere in what they undertake.' He commuted weekly between Serampore and Calcutta; leaving Serampore at 3pm on Tuesday and arriving back in time for evening tea on Friday. At Serampore his study was only a short distance away from the room where his wife Dorothy had to be confined and spent her days shouting and calling out, sometimes obscenities. His mind no doubt was as sad as hers was disturbed. There was to be no happy ending to Dorothy's story; having slept for most of the final two weeks of her life, she died on Tuesday 8 December 1807. William wrote, 'This evening Mrs. Carey died of the fever under which she has languished some time. Her death was a very easy one; but there was no appearance of returning reason, nor any thing that could cast a dawn of hope or light on her state.' Dorothy's moving story is a tragic one of a wife and mother who sacrificed personal comfort to be with her husband on the mission field, but who never here enjoyed the fruit of her costly sacrifice.

Just six months later, after

dealing with some stern objections from his fellow missionaries, on 8 May 1808, William remarried. He was never one to let people hinder him from what his heart was set on. His new wife was Charlotte Rumohr, a forty-six year old Danish lady whom he had begun teaching English in November 1800, and whom he had baptised back in June 1803 and who, despite very fragile physical health, was a robust supporter of the mission and a great help to William. They were deeply attached to one another, and had thirteen very happy years together. After her death, in May 1821, William wrote, 'We had as great a share of happiness as ever was enjoyed by mortals.' In his will, he left instructions that he was to be buried in Serampore graveyard next to his second wife.

And yet in September 1823 Carey married for a third time! Grace Hughes was seventeen years younger than William, and he found in her a 'most gentle and affectionate partner.' Like Dorothy and Charlotte before her, she was unbaptised when she married William, but like Dorothy and Charlotte he baptised her too.

Other trials and storms came the way of the mission in the form of opposition both in India and at home in England—even in parliament itself; but by the grace of God Carey and his team weathered them all. They even lost their money in some major bank crashes during 1830 and 1831, causing serious concern about the ongoing work of Serampore and the mission stations. But they held on, trusted God, and refused to recall any of the missionaries they had sent out to the mission stations.

A star that shone brightly

There was just no quitting for Carey, Marshman, Ward and others on their team—only forward and onward. It was

Above: Carey aged 60

Top: The inscription on the grave of Carey's second wife Charlotte, and third wife Grace

Above: An old colonial building in Calcutta

especially Carey who was the man who would not quit. Certainly this was his character, but it was strengthened by his unwavering belief in God's character and promises.

In 1832, the fortieth year of the Mission, Carey and Marshman were reflecting on what God had done during the past four decades. It was an amazing story. Great things had been expected from God—great things had been attempted—great things had been done. Greater perhaps than they first imagined; they were like men who dreamed: 'Look at what God has done through us'. And Carey stated that he had 'scarcely a wish ungratified.'

Throughout the years of 1833 and 1834 Carey's health fluctuated wildly; sometimes he was speechless and so weak that those around him thought he was dying; but Carey frequently rallied and recovered. Eventually he had to give in and at 5:30am on Monday 9 June 1834, he breathed his final breath on earth and then took his place in glory alongside those from every nation, tribe, people and language before the throne of God; learning the language of heaven in an instant. His body was buried in Serampore graveyard with his own choice of words from an Isaac Watts hymn: 'A wretched, poor and helpless worm, On thy kind arms I fall.'

At one point during his time in India, when he was facing endless opposition and discouragement, someone asked him if it was all worth it, and he replied, 'But when it shall be said, the infamous

The difference Carey made to India

In their book, *Carey, Christ and Cultural Transformation*, Ruth and Vishal Mangalwadi have a whole chapter showing how William Carey was the central character in the story of the modernization of India. Here are some of the examples they give:

To the sciences: he introduced the Linnaean system to botany and published the first books on science and natural history in India.

To mechanical engineering: he introduced the steam engine to India.

To economics: he introduced the idea of Savings Banks.

To the medical world: he campaigned for the humane treatment of lepers.

To the print world: he built, what was then, the largest press in India.

To the publishing world: he printed the first newspaper in any oriental language.

To agriculture: he founded the Agri-Horticultural Society to maximise usage of the land.

To literature: he translated and published some great Indian classics such as the *Ramayana*, and wrote the first Sanskrit dictionary for scholars.

To education: he started dozens of schools for Indian children of all castes.

To astronomy: he taught that the stars and planets were not deities that governed our lives, but created by God to help us keep time and to govern the world.

To the library: he introduced the idea of lending libraries.

To forest conservation: he taught and wrote about the cultivation and use of timber.

To the suppression of women: he stood against polygamy, female infanticide, child marriage, widow-burning, euthanasia and forced female illiteracy; and he positively opened schools for girls.

To the ethos of the British East India Company: through his position of professor in Fort William he influenced the British administration to move from imperial exploitation to a civil service.

Above: Carey's tomb in Serampore

swinging post is no longer erected; the widow burns no more on the funeral pyre; the obscene dances and songs are seen and heard no more; the gods are thrown to the bats, and Jesus is known as the God of the whole land; the Hindu goes no more to the Ganges to be washed from his uncleanness, but to the fountain opened for sin; and the crowds say, "Let us go up to the house of the Lord, and He shall teach us of His ways;" the anxious Hindus no more consume their property, their strength, and their lives in vain pilgrimages, but come at once to Him, Who can save to the

WILLIAM CAREY, D.D.

BORN: 17 AUGUST 1761

DIED: 9 JUNE 1834

A WRETCHED, POOR AND HELPLESS WORM

ON THY KIND ARMS I FALL

uttermost; the sick and the dying are no more dragged to the Ganges, but look to the Lamb of God, and commit their souls into His faithful hands; the children are no more sacrificed to idols, but are become "the seed of the Lord"; the public morals are improved; benevolent societies are formed; civilisation and salvation walk arm in arm together; the earth yields her increase; and innumerable souls from this vast country swell the chorus of the redeemed—shall we then think that we have laboured in vain?'

EDINBURGH

BELFAST

DUBLIN

PAULERSPURY
NORTHAMPTON
MOULTON

NOTTINGHAM

LEICESTER

KETTERING

CARDIFF

LONDON

UNITED KINGDOM AND EIRE

INDIA

MUDNABATTI
MALDA

WEST
BENGAL

BANDEL
SERAMPORE
DEBHATA
CALCUTTA

BAY OF BENGAL

Upon entering India Carey stayed in *Calcutta* for three weeks from 11 November to early December 1793.

He moved to *Bandel* in December 1793, staying until January 1794. Bandel, once an important port, is situated 30 miles north of Calcutta on the banks of the River Hooghly.

From mid January to early February 1794, he settled at *Maniktala*—now a busy part of Calcutta.

On 4 February 1794 he left Baliagut (near Manicktolla) and took a boat through the salt rivers arriving at *Debhata* in the Sundarbans two days later. Debhatta, now in Bangladesh, is 40 miles east of Calcutta.

Leaving Debhatta on 23 May 1794 he took a boat journey to *Malda,* arriving on 14 June 1794. Malda, 217 miles north of Calcutta, was at one time the capital of Bengal. *Mudnabatti,* the village where Carey settled, was 32 miles north of Malda up the Tangan River.

On 1 January 1800 he set out on a river journey to *Serampore* arriving on 10 January. Serampore was a Danish colony and is 12 miles due north of Calcutta.

A SUMMARY OF CAREY'S LIFE

17 August 1761	Born, Paulerspury, Northamptonshire
1775	Started work as a trainee shoemaker with Clarke Nichols
10 February 1779	First attends a Sunday meeting at Hackleton meeting-house.
5 October 1779	Enters the service of Thomas Old
19 May 1781	Joins with others in forming Hackleton Dissenting Church
10 June 1781	Married Dorothy Plackett at Piddington Church.
Summer 1782	Begins lay preaching at Earl's Barton Baptist meeting.
5 October 1783	Baptised in the River Nene by John Ryland Jr
Autumn 1783	Reads Captain Cook's Voyages and is inspired to missionary work.
25 March 1785	Moved to Moulton
20 October 1785	Felix Carey born
10 August 1786	Ordained by Olney Baptist church
1 August 1787	Officially starts at Moulton
October 1787	Dorothy Carey baptised
1788	William Junior born
1789	Peter born
July 1789	Moved to Leicester to become probationer pastor at Harvey Lane
September 1790	Dissolves church membership at Harvey Lane.
27 April 1791	Northamptonshire "Preaching Day" at Clipston.
24 May 1791	Probation finished; formally ordained to be pastor of Harvey Lane
12 May 1792	Publication of 'Enquiry …'
31 May 1792	Nottingham Assembly and Carey's deathless sermon
2 October 1792	The Missionary society founded at Widow Wallis' house in Kettering.
9 January 1793	Carey volunteers to go to Bengal with John Thomas
20 March 1793	Farewell service at Harvey Lane with Carey's fellow Baptist ministers
4 April 1793	Embark on Earl of Oxford for India.
1793	Six weeks delay on the Isle of Wight.
Early May 1793	Jabez Carey born
21 May 1793	Thrown off ship.
13 June 1793	Aboard The Kron Princessa Maria at Dover, bound for India
9 November 1793	Carey's first sight of and 'interview' with the Hindus
11 November 1793	Enters Calcutta and stays there for 3 weeks.
December 1793	Moves to Bandel
By 13 January 1794	Living in Maniktala
6 February 1794	Living in Debhatta, Sundarbans.
4 August 1794	Family move into new home in Mudnabatti.

11 October 1794	5 year old Peter dies from malaria
9 May 1795	First letters arrive from England
October 1795	Translates Genesis, Exodus, Matthew, parts of James and John into Bengali
January 1796	Jonathan Carey born
May 1799	Filled with horror as he witnessed sati
13 October 1799	Missionaries Ward, Marshman, Brunsdon and Grant (and families) and Miss Tidd land in India only to be impounded in Serampore!
10 January 1800	Arrives in Serampore
24 April 1800	Thanksgiving service for the completion of school building at Serampore
May 1800	Mission Press prints first leaf of Carey's Bengali New Testament
28 December 1800	Double baptism of Felix Carey and Krishna Pal
5 March 1801	The first Bengali NT published and placed on the communion table
April 1801	Becomes Tutor in Bengali at Fort William college
13 October 1801	John Thomas dies
1804	By this year infanticide had been wiped out mainly due to Carey's work
1804	First of 19 mission stations established
1806	Joins the Asiatic Society
26 August 1806	Carey instructed by Supreme court to cease from preaching to Indians
1807	Conferred with a doctorate from Brown's University, Providence, USA.
8 December 1807	Dorothy Carey dies
9 May 1808	Marries Charlotte Rumohr
1808	Sanskrit New Testament published
1 January 1809	Opening of Lall Bazar Chapel
11 March 1812	The fire in Serampore
15 July 1818	Prospectus issued for Serampore college
14 September 1820	Founded the Agricultural and Horticultural Society of India
30 May 1821	Carey's second wife, Charlotte, dies
7 March 1823	William Ward dies of cholera
1823	Carey becomes a fellow of the Linnaean Society.
1823	Late summer Marries Grace Hughes
17 March 1827	The break with the home committee (BMS) and society
1827	The College is granted the power to confer divinity degrees by the King of Denmark.
December 1829	Sati abolished! Legislation on 4th, translation on the 6th
June 1830	Carey pensioned off from Fort William college in cut backs.
1832	Eighth and final revision of the Bengali NT.
9 June 1834	William Carey dies at sunrise.

Further Reading

William Carey, *An Enquiry into the obligation etc.*, Ann Ireland, Leicester, 1792.

Ruth and Vishal Mangalwadi, *Carey, Christ and Cultural Transformation*, OM Publishing 1997. ISBN 1 85078 258 x

James R Beck, *Dorothy Carey—The tragic and untold story of Mrs William Carey*, Wipf and Stock Publishers, 2000. ISBN: 1 57910 341 3

Timothy George, *Faithful Witness—The Life and Mission of William Carey*, IVP 1992. ISBN 0 85110 980 2

Michael A.G. Haykin, *One Heart and One Soul—John Sutcliff of Olney, his friends and his times*, Evangelical Press, 1994. ISBN 0 85234 326 4

S Pearce-Carey, William Carey, Wakeman Trust, London, 1993. ISBN 1 870855 14 0

About the Author

Paul Pease is married to Rosemarie and they have three daughters, Ellen, Bethany and Anna. Paul became a Christian whilst working on a local newspaper in Bournemouth and soon after began a two year study period at Moorlands Bible College. After further study at The London Theological Seminary he became pastor of West Kilburn Baptist Church, London, for thirteen years. In 1997 Paul moved to Hook Evangelical Church, Surbiton, where he now serves as pastor. His interests mainly revolve around family but he watches AFC Bournemouth whenever possible!

Acknowledgements

The informative and enthusiastic Margaret Williams who has helped no end in providing me with details and access to the Carey museum in Moulton.

The energetic and friendly Mollie Dunkerly, in Paulerspury who goes about her duties so cheerfully.

Rev. Dr Peter Shepherd for permission to use his photographs of Serampore.

Vishal Mangalwandi for his time and inspirational insight into Carey's big vision.

Liz Chang for her Latin translation.

Dr Michael Haykin for reading through the mss, his helpful insights, suggestions, and photographs.

Shirley Shire, Librarian at Bristol Baptist College for her enthusiasm and delight to serve.

Jyoti Chakravatty for photographs and local knowledge of Calcutta and Serampore.